A DOCUMENTARY HISTORY
OF THE
FAITH AND ORDER MOVEMENT
1927–1963

A DOCUMENTARY HISTORY OF THE FAITH AND ORDER MOVEMENT 1927-1963

Edited by

LUKAS VISCHER

THE BETHANY PRESS

St. Louis, Missouri

Manufactured in the United States of America

CONTENTS

ABBREVIATIONS

Am   Amsterdam Assembly _____ See pp.   75 ff.

Ed   Edinburgh Conference _____ See pp.   40 ff.

Ev   Evanston Assembly _____ See pp. 131 ff.

La   Lausanne Conference _____ See pp.   27 ff.

Lu   Lund Conference _____ See pp.   85 ff.

ND   New Delhi Assembly _____ See pp. 144 ff.

Pr   Proselytism and Religious Liberty _____ See pp. 183 ff.

Ro   Rolle Statement _____ See pp. 177 ff.

To   Toronto Statement _____ See pp. 167 ff.

INTRODUCTION

Faith and Order Reports:

Their Nature

and Significance

The beginnings of the Faith and Order movement lie already in the distant past. The number of those who were present at the first conferences is constantly dwindling, and many of those who take part in theological discussions today are barely acquainted with the history of the early decades. It happens time and again that such conversation is carried on without knowledge of earlier discussions, and not everyone is aware that our deliberations today are continuous with a movement which began over fifty years ago. It may be well, therefore, to make the most important documents generally accessible in one volume. This collection contains the reports of the three World Conferences on Faith and Order; the reports of the Assemblies of the World Council of Churches insofar as they relate to the concerns of the Faith and Order movement; statements of the Central Committee of the World Council of Churches; and some other documents. True, these documents are not sufficient to provide the reader with a picture of the movement which is complete in every detail. To obtain this he would have to refer in addition to the literature which is listed at the end of this volume. But the collection is sufficiently complete to reveal in broad outline the development of the theological questioning and seeking which has been going on in the framework of the Faith and Order movement, and thus to show the context in which the present conversations exist and in which they must be continued.

Reports of ecumenical conferences are documents of a rather special kind. They have been produced under special conditions and circumstances and can really be understood only by someone who is aware of these. As soon as they are regarded apart from the movement of which they are the expression, their meaning and significance are no longer clear, and false criteria are inevitably applied to them. It is important, therefore, that we should realize the origin and special nature of this ecumenical literature. Only then can the question be answered as to how far the reports of these conferences are significant for the Christian churches participating in the ecumenical movement.

1. Let us first call to mind the historical circumstances which underlie the reports of the Faith and Order movement and thus a large portion of modern ecumenical literature. They owe their origin to the fact that at the beginning of this century the question of the unity of the Church of Christ emerged in a new way and with new urgency. The yearning that the Church of Christ, which after all by its very nature can be only one, should appear as one, admittedly did not emerge for the first time in this century. The Christian churches have always prayed for true unity in Christ. In all ages figures have arisen who have recognized their special call to the service of unity, and time and again movements for the recovery of unity have arisen. But the movement in our century is distinguished by a special factor. The state of division has become so intolerable to the separated Christian churches that they have started a conversation which is increasingly *systematic*, and they have also begun more and more to *act together*. In contrast with numerous earlier efforts towards unity, the modern ecumenical movement does not consist in an appeal to the churches to overcome the differences which separate them on the basis of a certain predetermined understanding of unity. Rather, the churches have resolved, on the basis of their common origin in Christ, to enter into conversation with one another, and in the framework of this tentative fellowship to seek the way to greater unity and to follow this way as it may be revealed and opened to them by God.

The resolution which constituted the beginning of the Faith and Order movement is significant in this respect. The General Synod of the Protestant Episcopal Church in the United States adopted the following resolution in 1910: "Whereas there is today among all Christian people a growing desire for the fulfillment of our Lord's prayer that all his disciples may be one; that the world may believe that God has sent him; Resolved, the House of Bishops concurring, that a Joint Committee be appointed to bring about a conference for the considerations of questions touching Faith and Order and all *Christian Communions throughout the world which confess our Lord Jesus Christ as God and Saviour* be asked to unite with us in arranging

8

for and conducting such a conference."[1] In this resolution all the important features which characterize the Faith and Order movement are already included. The churches which have Christ as God and Saviour at the center of their being are invited to enter into conversation with one another. By taking this step they establish a certain fellowship amongst themselves. For the sake of their common Lord they at least take one another seriously enough to meet together and to subject to re-examination the relationship which they have one to another. They are prepared to allow themselves to be confronted with each other's confessions and church life. And so genuine fellowship has come about; for in that the churches are prepared to do this, they begin to set upon one another in a new way, and the longer the conversation lasts, the closer this fellowship becomes. The division which exists is not thereby removed, it is true. The boundaries do not become blurred. The churches remain true to their own confessions. Only while still in their state of division they have entered upon a new relationship with one another.

The reports which have been produced in the Faith and Order movement clearly reflect this initial situation. In both content and form they are marked by the tension between unity and division. They attest on the one hand that unity is given in Christ. They show that on the basis of this unity the churches are in a position to speak with a common voice. We have only to think of the sections in which common convictions are formulated or where at any rate an attempt is made to formulate them. We would think particularly of the messages which have come out of individual conferences, and in which the churches are called to give increased expression to their unity in Christ. But on the other hand the reports also reveal the profound and unresolved differences which separate the churches one from another. For the reports do not confine themselves to reproducing the points of agreement. From the very beginning one of the basic principles of the movement has been that differences, too, must be reported in all sincerity. And frequently even the agreements say so little and are phrased so vaguely that they are evidence less of unity than of division. A well-known example which is frequently quoted with irony is the first sentence which the Section on the Gospel in Lausanne (1927) managed to formulate: "the message of the church to the world is and must always remain the Gospel of Jesus Christ."[2] Frequently, too,

[1]Cf. Joint Commission appointed to arrange for a World Conference on Faith and Order. Faith and Order paper 2, p. 3.
[2]See Lausanne 9.

9

agreements rest upon carefully thought-out formulations which, although able to be accepted in one way or another by all those present, nevertheless have different meanings for different people. The agreement exists then in the words, it is true, but not, or at best only imperfectly, in the matter itself, and an experienced person recognises immediately how much precisely such sentences as these are an expression of continuing profound division. It would be wrong to talk of insincerity in this connection. When churches separated from one another enter into conversation, they are *bound* to arrive at formulations of this kind. Verbal agreement defines to a certain extent the area within which the churches with their differing conceptions have to meet together. Although it does not represent a genuine consensus and must not be misunderstood as such, it nevertheless represents a certain framework within which the conversation can be continued. The tension between fellowship and division finds particularly clear expression, therefore, precisely in this characteristic of the conference reports.

2. When we say that in the Faith and Order movement the churches have entered upon a relationship of systematic theological conversation with one another, we must add immediately that this conversation has its own internal dynamics. The conversation does not consist of individual unrelated encounters. In allowing themselves to be invited to a conference on questions of faith and order, the churches took a momentous step. The preparation and holding of the first conference bound the churches so strongly together that it became absolutely necessary for the conversation to be carried further. The conclusions which had been reached had to be evaluated and clarified further, and the increased opportunities for theological discussion had to be exploited. It was natural, therefore, that after some time a second world conference should be planned, and it has remained until today a characteristic feature of the Faith and Order movement that after the lapse of several years an invitation to a fresh world conference goes out. Lausanne (1927) was followed by Edinburgh (1937); after the second world war the series was continued with Lund (1952), and Montreal (1963).

These conferences have a double task. In the first place they serve to draw together the results of the ecumenical theological conversation. The delegates seek to formulate both the progress and the difficulties which have resulted from the encounter

10

between the churches. In this way they render an account of the state of the conversation both to themselves and to the churches involved in the movement. But this joint backward glance is not the sole purpose of the world conferences. They also serve as an occasion for self-examination. The delegates have to ask themselves what steps the churches can take today on the basis of the present situation and what steps ought to be aimed at and achieved. They have to attempt to ascertain and describe the problems which obstruct the path of the churches toward greater unity and which therefore demand to be dealt with specially in a common endeavour. Time and again the world conferences have proved to be an opportunity for imparting a common direction to the formulation of theological questions, and in this way they have contributed to the co-ordination of the churches' theological work.

We can see then that theological conversation in the Faith and Order movement proceeds with a special rhythm. A world conference recapitulates what has been done and makes suggestions for the future. The report of the conference is taken up and discussed in many individual encounters and conversations of the most diverse kinds. Certain suggestions are carried out, and certain questions are brought closer to being answered by means of careful work performed by specially appointed theological commissions. Occasionally it turns out that the report of the conference did not really go to the heart of the matter. Disagreement arises, and fresh points of view are added; and at the same time the general theological work advances. New results come to light, and frequently historical events and convulsions help to bring it about that the theological problems are viewed and answered in a fresh way in the individual churches. We think, for example, of the significance of the two world wars for theological thinking. All these individual endeavours find expression in the preparatory material for a fresh world conference. On the basis of the experience which has been gained an attempt is made to find a fresh formulation for the theological problems of unity and to indicate those places where new possibilities are opening up for the conversation between the churches. As a result of discussion and comment upon these preparatory reports in the churches, additional points of view are brought in, and the conference is thus in a position to discuss these ecumenical questions on a fresh basis.

Corresponding to this rhythm, different groups of ecumenical literature can be distinguished within the Faith and Order move-

11

ment. In the first place there is of course the *general literature* on the problems of faith and order: writings and statements of individual theologians which have an important bearing on the question of church unity, reports of meetings, of conferences large or small, of individual groups who have worked together on a specific subject in its relation to unity in Christ. Many of these publications have only a loose and remote connection with the organised Faith and Order movement, others have originated in one way or another through its work or have even been produced directly within its framework. To be distinguished from this general writing is that literature which is directly connected with a world conference. There is first the *preparatory material* which is produced with a world conference in view. This consists chiefly of reports and proposals which are intended to serve as information, stimulation, and basis of discussion for the delegates. Then there is the *report* proper, which is produced during the conference itself. Up to now it has always been published together with the minutes of the proceedings, so that it should not be understood as an isolated document but should be read in the context of the situation. And finally there is the literature which concerns itself with the *results of a conference*. It consists of accounts, articles, essays, and so forth, and has so many ramifications that it can hardly be grasped in its totality. In some cases an attempt has been made to give a summary of the reactions to a world conference.

But in simply describing the rhythm in which the theological conversation in the Faith and Order movement proceeds from one conference to the next, we have by no means as yet fully grasped the internal dynamics of the movement. Malicious tongues will always say, of course, that the movement is nothing but an international exchange of views organised at great expense, a noncommittal encounter between theologians from various countries, which may well stimulate and foster theological thinking, but leaves no real traces in the lives of the various churches. And without a doubt this reproach must be taken seriously. When one sees the flood of books, articles, and essays which have been produced in the last few decades in the context of Faith and Order, one must indeed ask oneself what results have emerged from all these strenuous efforts. Are we not in fact spending our days "as idle talk"? Are we not in fact going round and round the same questions without coming any nearer to a solution of *the* essential question which gave rise to the movement? When we look at the texts more closely, however, we

12

do find that undeniable progress has been made. The futility of many endeavours may be obvious, and a person who has recognised the urgency of the task can hardly avoid growing impatient. But there can be no doubt that the continued theological conversation has strengthened and deepened the fellowship between the churches. The discussions may revert time and again to the same problems; but it is obvious that the assumptions on which the conversation is based have altered perceptibly in the course of the decades. The unity which binds the churches together is more clearly conceived, and the questions which are asked have become in far greater measure questions which are common to all.

3. The progress of the movement can be recognised, for example, in the way in which with the passage of the years the method of theological conversation has changed. The conference at Lausanne (1927) declared in its report: "We . . . are assembled to consider the things wherein we agree and the things wherein we differ."[3] The immediate concern, then, was simply to get to know one another in a direct encounter and to work out together what bound the churches to one another and what divided them, so that the churches might no longer view one another on the basis of prejudice, caricature, or even illusion, but might really comprehend their relationship to one another. The conversation concentrated upon an attempt to set side by side the various "convictions" and to formulate as precisely as possible what relationship they bore to one another. This method was necessary to begin with; for it had first to be made clear what reality the individual churches have in mind when they defend this or that conviction, and the concepts which they use had to be clarified. But was it possible for this method to prove satisfactory in the long run? Was it possible really to overcome the differences in this way? On the contrary, were not the contradictions becoming more profound as a result of constant comparison? Did not this sort of conversation actually compel the churches to lay stress upon the particularities which distinguished them from other churches? There can be no doubt that in fact the theological conversation between the confessions has led to a revival of confessional consciousness in many churches. But could the matter be left there? Was it not necessary to find ways by which the established confessional boundaries could be penetrated? The discussions at the Second World Conference in Edinburgh were still largely determined by the method of com-

[3]See La 1.

13

parison. After the second world war, however, this method predominated less and less. At Amsterdam an attempt was still made to define which among the numerous individual differences was the "deepest difference" dividing the churches, and it was thought that this difference could be described in the key words "catholic" and "protestant."[4] But already at Lund the method of ecumenical conversation was determined in a different way. "We have seen clearly that we can make no real advance toward unity if we only compare our several conceptions of the nature of the church and the traditions in which they are embodied. . . . We need to penetrate behind our divisions to a deeper and richer understanding of the mystery of the God-given union of Christ with his Church. We need increasingly to realize that the separate histories of our churches find their full meaning only if seen in the perspective of God's dealings with his whole people."[5] This statement is of far-reaching importance. For it alters, so to speak, the perspective. Whereas up till then the churches had stood confronting one another, now a common point of view had been achieved which gave the necessary direction to their conversation. The unity given in Christ was no longer simply the subject of a solemn joint declaration, but had rather become the point of departure for common reflection. The churches resolved to consider primarily the "mysterious union of Christ with his Church," and to subordinate their deliberations to this reality to which they together bore witness. True, there is a wide divergence between them in their understanding of unity. The union of Christ with his people is the bond which holds them together; but it is obscured and concealed under numerous differences to which the churches are in conscience bound and which they cannot therefore pass over. Thus they have as yet no common access to that true unity to which they nevertheless bear common witness. And yet the character of their conversation changes if they take this as their starting point and endeavour together to gain a fresh understanding of the unity which is given by God. They no longer meet in order to fix the limits dividing them one from another; on the contrary, they have been introduced to a common process of questioning. They no longer ask primarily what are the features which distinguish them from other churches, but seek rather to see the differences which separate them in the light of their common relationship to the living Lord of the Church, and there can be no

[4] See Am 5-8.
[5] See Lu 2.

14

doubt that as a result many questions involuntarily take on a different aspect. Many of the studies undertaken after Lund are clear proof of this.

4. Closely connected with the change in method is the fact that it has proved possible to achieve important progress in another respect also. Whereas in earlier times it seemed impossible to define the unity which the churches were endeavoring to manifest amongst themselves, the attempt has recently been made to arrive at a common definition, and it looks as though certain obstacles which formerly appeared insuperable have gradually dwindled in importance. We have already seen that the founders of the Faith and Order movement deliberately refrained from making one particular conception of unity a condition of cooperation. The aim was rather to draw the churches into conversation, and the question as to what kind of unity was in accordance with the will of God was to be one of the subjects of this conversation. This decision was taken not just for practical reasons but sprang from the recognition that the conception of unity was indissolubly bound up with the doctrinal teaching of the individual churches and that therefore an agreement could only be worked out in conversation together. The question was then in fact repeatedly taken up, but at first only served to reveal the great difficulties relating to it. At Lausanne an attempt was made to enumerate the marks of the true Church. It was declared emphatically "that the one life of the one body should be manifest to the world."[6] But at the same time it was set forth in some detail that the question of the visible or invisible nature of the Church presented insoluble difficulties, and it is clear that in this, of all questions, a certain agreement is essential if that unity which the churches have to manifest amongst themselves is to be defined. At Edinburgh similar difficulties revealed themselves. The report distinguishes three different forms of church unity: co-operative action, intercommunion, and organic union.[7] But the conference was clearly not in a position to state which of these three forms represented the common end to be striven for. Individual delegates declared explicitly, for example, that "federal union is not only the most we can achieve but also the most we should desire," a declaration which was obviously directed against the idea of organic union. And after the second world war progress was not immediately possible. After the formation of the World Council

[6]See La 22.
[7]See Edi 113-126.

of Churches it was doubly important to take seriously and in all frankness the profound differences between the churches. Thus the Toronto statement says expressly: ". . . but none of these conceptions [of unity] can be called the ecumenical theory. The whole point of the ecumenical conversation is precisely that all these conceptions enter into dynamic relations with each other."[8] But after Lund the situation soon changed. After so much emphasis had been placed upon statements about the unity given in Christ, it was natural that the churches should once more turn together to the question of the way in which this unity could be given expression in accordance with the will of Christ. The fruit of this endeavour is the definition of unity which was accepted by the New Delhi Assembly. The text enumerates the matters in which the church must be one so that the unity given in Christ may become visible. True, this enumeration does not yet represent any complete agreement. Many questions relating to the unity given in Christ remain unanswered, and above all it must be noted that the churches are still far from understanding in the same way those marks of unity listed in the definition. And yet this text contains a number of significant statements. By contrast with earlier times, it is now clearly stated that unity must find visible expression and that all in each place who are baptized into the name of Christ must grow into a single fully committed fellowship. The will to visible unity has obviously become the common will of the churches.

5. But, finally, the progress of the movement can be recognised from the fact that the continuity of the conversation from one conference to another has taken on an increasingly binding character. Let us recall especially in this connection the setting up of the World Council of Churches in 1948. It is clear that the formation of a permanent fellowship between the churches means that the theological conversation has become more binding in character. Therefore the Faith and Order movement has changed through its integration into the World Council. To begin with, it was solely a matter of drawing representatives of the individual churches into conversation. In this the churches took upon themselves only a limited mutual obligation. But in agreeing at Edinburgh in 1937 to the formation of a World Council of Churches, the representatives of the churches took an important step forward. By this decision they made it clear that the encounter had become a real commitment. From now on the churches were living together. They no longer approached

[8]See To 7.

16

one another as totally separate bodies, but began to act together and to manifest their unity to the world. In consequence their theological conversation acquired an urgency which it did not have before.

Thus, since the formation of the World Council of Churches, the conversation has been carried on much more intensively. The questions which had arisen for treatment in the Faith and Order movement are now discussed at the Assemblies and the meetings of the Central Committee as well, and in addition to the documents of the Faith and Order movement there are now the reports of the Assemblies and the statements of the Central Committee. The conversation is taking place on two levels, and it is clear that this has made possible not only a quicker pace but also a greater measure of participation by the churches.

The reports of the Assemblies are of a characteristically different kind from those of the Faith and Order conferences. As a rule they deal with the large general problems which arise in connection with unity. They present focal points and suggestions, rather than going into the details of theological discussion. They are certainly also more representative, and there can be no doubt that more weight attaches to the theological statements of an Assembly than to those of other conferences. In relation to the Assemblies and the work of the Central Committee, the world conferences and Commission meetings of Faith and Order are in the nature of preparatory work. Their task is to clarify the theological problems of unity in such a way that the churches can move forward on the path to unity.

The Faith and Order movement has not simply been absorbed into the World Council of Churches, however. On the contrary, at the time of the Council's formation great importance was attached to its retaining a certain measure of independence; the special concerns out of which it had grown were not to be lost. Thus, although the movement has been incorporated into the World Council of Churches, it has at the same time maintained a certain autonomy. A special "Commission on Faith and Order" was formed, which was to be responsible for carrying on the work, and it was clear from the outset that even after the formation of the World Council of Churches the series of world conferences on Faith and Order should be continued. The special position of the Commission on Faith and Order is indicated particularly by the fact that it is composed not only of representatives of member chuches, but always includes representatives of other churches as well. It is intended that the theo-

17

logical conversation on unity in Christ should continue to be as broadly based as possible, and for this reason churches which cannot, or cannot yet, decide to enter into membership of the World Council should not be excluded from this conversation.

It was undoubtedly a wise decision not to allow the movement to be completely absorbed into the World Council of Churches. The theological conversation follows its own laws and needs independence and freedom in order to be able to develop in accordance with its own character. It must certainly take place within the context of the living fellowship of the churches, but it must not come to be dominated by practical and pragmatic considerations. Therefore the Faith and Order movement can best fulfil its function if it is allowed to retain a certain, if limited, amount of autonomy. It is then in the best position to take up the problems raised through the churches' living together, and then in turn pass on to the fellowship of the churches the benefit of its work. The special position occupied by the Faith and Order movement in the structure of the World Council of Churches corresponds in a way to the special position which should be accorded to theology in the church as a whole, and the progress of the movement can be ascertained not least from the fact that the churches have agreed to give it this important place in their common life.

6. If we say that the fellowship between the separated churches has deepened with the passage of the years and that agreement in important questions has grown, a further question inevitably arises. Can one say that a certain degree of authority, even if only a limited degree, attaches to the reports which have been produced in the context of the Faith and Order movement? Can it be said, for example, that the declarations of an Assembly or a world conference on Faith and Order give a reliable picture of the agreement existing among the churches? Can it be said that they are in any way binding upon the churches? Or are they intended simply as the results of discussion at a large-scale conference, which the churches may or may not use according to their needs? Opinions vary on this question. Sometimes the reports are spoken of as though they represented an ecumenical consensus of opinion amongst the churches and were therefore to a large extent binding upon the churches. Many who are moved by the miracle of the ecumenical movement incline to this view. Others, on the contrary, see in these reports nothing more than documents which may be read with profit as ex-

18

pressions of the ecumenical conversation, but can claim no authority in themselves. What can one say about this?

We have already seen that the reports arising out of the Faith and Order movement are marked both in content and in form by the tension between unity and division in which the Christian churches live. It follows inevitably that they are somewhat indefinite in character. A conference on Faith and Order does not meet in order to come to a decision on the questions which are put to it. It is not a council, either in the sense of the ecumenical councils of the Early Church, or in the sense of the papal councils, even if it has sometimes been described as a council.[9] It meets in order to ascertain what agreement exists amongst the separated Churches, and to deepen the fellowship amongst them by common discussion of important questions. Thus the reports are from the outset only provisional in character. They are no more than a first attempt to formulate a consensus, and it must then be shown in the conversation of the churches *themselves* whether this formulation corresponds to the actual facts. Almost all the reports are introduced by the phrase "received and commended for consideration to the Churches *nemine contradicente.*" But this means it is made quite clear that they are intended to be no more than proposals or suggestions.

Let us take an example to make this clear. At the Edinburgh conference (1937) the question of grace and justification was under discussion. To the great surprise of all the participants a successful attempt was made to work out a text which met with general acceptance.[10] When the agreement was achieved, the conference was greatly moved. Those present rose spontaneously to give thanks to God. An important obstacle seemed to have been removed. And yet the report was to prove unable to obtain the assent of the churches. Many expressed reservations and asserted that important aspects had been ignored. The report can therefore count in only a very limited sense as a consensus, and we can see that the weight attaching to a report depends upon the extent to which it is approved by the churches. The reports of the Faith and Order movement—whether they be declarations of an Assembly or of a world conference—cannot therefore claim any authority for themselves as such. Their whole authority lies in the wisdom inherent in them, and if we want to find out whether they represent a consensus of opinion in the

[9]W. Elert called the Lausanne conference a church council. Cf. E. Schlink: *Oekumenische Konzile einst und heute*, in *Der kommende Christus und die kirchlichen Traditionen*, 1961, and *Ecumenical Review* XIV, 3, April 1962, pp. 281 ff.
[10]See Ed. 2-18.

churches, we must ask how the churches received them. And indeed it is necessary to keep on asking this question, for it can be that a report which is at first received favorably appears a few years later in another light. The ecumenical movement is a dynamic movement. New churches are constantly coming into it, with new insights, and the churches which have taken part in it from the beginning do not remain the same. Therefore it can very easily come about that a report which to begin with appeared to be pertinent and exhaustive has later to be re-worked in the light of fresh points of view. This tentativeness is one of the marks of the common journey toward unity which God has prepared for His people in Christ. Nor in this connection must we overlook the fact that the reports do not even rest upon the complete agreement of the conference themselves. The phrase *"nemine contradicente"* is a negative one. It does not say that those present have given their assent to every part, but only that they have found no reason expressly to dissociate themselves from it. It is therefore quite possible that even amongst the participants at a conference many reservations may remain, and many may have refrained from expressing disagreement because the reports were in any case intended only for study in the churches. In this connection we must call to mind especially the Orthodox participants. Often indeed they have expressed their reservations openly. At Lund the Orthodox group had it recorded in the minutes that they had abstained from voting. At Evanston the Orthodox delegates drew up a detailed separate statement, and even at New Delhi there was talk at least of a similar state-ment. It is therefore obvious that a report may not be regarded automatically as an expression of complete agreement.

But is that all that can be said about the meaning and author-ity of these reports? Must we be content with these qualifying remarks? Or must we on the contrary, having made these qualifi-cations, look at the whole question again from another point of view? Necessary as it is to exclude from the outset any idea of an external authority possessed by the reports, it would neverthe-less be wrong to regard them simply as the products of discus-sion at a conference. This interpretation would not take sufficient account of the fact that in beginning a systematic theological conversation in the Faith and Order movement, and above all in later forming the World Council, the churches have entered in-to a mutual obligation. They no longer stand alongside each other without mutual commitment. They have at least decided to recognise and accept the other Christian churches as permanent partners in the conversation. In so doing they have entered into a living fellowship, and it is obvious that this fellowship has a determining influence on all the churches. Ecumenical gatherings are therefore not the same as any other conferences. *They are rather the expression of the permanent living fellowship amongst the churches and represent to the individual churches the fellowship to which they have committed themselves.* For this reason the churches cannot possibly be simply spectators of the results of these gatherings. If this were so, they would not only be despising the fellowship of the churches but would also be failing to take seriously their own decision to belong to it. The decision to belong to the fellowship of churches who are engaged in conversation with one another obliges them, on the contrary, to regard the statements of representative ecumenical gatherings as their own business.

All important ecumenical gatherings are composed primarily of delegates who have been officially nominated by the churches. Thus they are not merely organised gatherings, but are convened on behalf of the churches themselves, and by sending their delegates the churches testify that they expect from the deliberations of the conference a clarification of certain issues. Most churches call upon their congregations to pray for the conference, and when an ecumenical gathering takes place, thousands pray that it may be led by the Holy Spirit. Therefore the participants, too, know that they have not come together in order to debate, but in order to obtain together a fresh and deeper knowledge of the Word of God. And if we really pray for true knowledge, do we not then also expect it to be given to us? We tend so much to cast doubt on the validity of all church activity that we are tempted in the process to forget the promise of the Holy Spirit. And yet we can have confidence that God will show us His way—even above all that we ask or think.

Does not all this impart a certain authority to the declarations which an ecumenical gathering succeeds in working out? Are not the churches at least placed under an obligation to subject them to a frank and thorough examination, even if they appear to the churches to be strange and questionable at first? The churches do not all look upon the obligation in the same way. True, they are willing to be informed about these matters, and as a rule encourage their members to discuss the reports. But it still happens too rarely that they voice an official opinion, that they express their agreement and draw the consequences for doctrine and order, or that they give notice of their reservations and propose better wordings. It does happen, certainly, and an increasing number of churches are creating the organs to take over this task. But on the whole the reports are still only discussed in print, and the discussion does not really affect the life of the churches themselves. Is not this basically a sign that the churches underestimate the fellowship in which they are already joined together? They are bound to one another and increasingly subject to a common influence. But they do not make the effort which is necessary in order to grasp this community intellectually and to express it in doctrine and order. The churches' obligation really to allow the reports to speak to them, and to respond to them, cannot therefore be sufficiently underlined. The answers ought to come in such a way that the ecumenical situation makes itself felt, and it ought to be self-evident that a church which does not express an opinion declares itself tacitly in agreement with the reports which have been submitted to it.

7. We come now to a final reflection. It has become clear to us several times already that the reports of the Faith and Order movement have an inherently provisional character. Admittedly they are signs of hope, if we look at them from the point of view of our common path to more perfect unity in Christ. Every formulation agreed upon jointly, however modest it may be, signifies a small step upon this path. But precisely on account of their imperfection, the reports at the same time remind us how far we still are from one another.

It is not difficult to point out the shortcomings of ecumenical theological work. For people possessed of a sarcastic vein a wide field is opened up here. But anyone who talks about the unsatisfactory aspects of ecumenical thinking must be fully aware that in so doing he is talking not only about the ecumenical movement, but at the same time about the churches themselves. Fundamentally, the tension which is characteristic of ecumenical work is also to be encountered again, in a different form, in the individual churches, and the theological statements of ecumenical gatherings, with all their shortcomings, reflect a problem which presents itself, though in a different way, in each individual church. We find ecumenical reports lacking in penetrating insight and lucid formation. So many contradictions and difficulties remain that no real testimony is achieved. It is therefore clear that the mandate and task of confessing and bearing witness to the truth of Christ in the absoluteness of its claim lies now as always with the individual churches. For it cannot be that the proclamation of the Gospel should be "suspended" until the churches have achieved unity. But can a church, after being in fellowship with other churches, still confess in exactly the same way the truth which has been entrusted to it? Is not its confession called in question by this fellowship? Does it not confess the truth in the awareness and hope that one day a common confession will be granted to a Christianity which is at present divided? At all events, the confession of each individual church also has a provisional character—even if this is so in a different way and to a different extent for each church.

It is not easy to stand firm in face of this tension between the growing fellowship amongst Christians and the task of each individual church. The demands are great, and therefore there is an obvious temptation to evade them. Various possibilities present themselves. One can propagate an ecumenical attitude in which the question concerning the truth is no longer asked at all, or one can hide once more behind the confessional walls. One can take refuge in ecumenical slogans or indulge in malicious criticism. When one considers this tension, one can really be assailed by a desperate feeling that there is no way out. But is that all? The tension also has its promise for everyone who knows that the Heavenly Father will *give* the Holy Spirit to those who ask Him, and therefore it is worth standing firm.

Lukas Vischer

I

Reports of World Conferences

1.

LAUSANNE

First World Conference
on Faith and Order
August 3-21, 1927

FINAL REPORT
PREAMBLE

Unanimously adopted by the full Conference

1   We, representatives of many Christian Communions throughout the world, united in the common confession of faith in Jesus Christ the Son of God, our Lord and Saviour, believing that the Spirit of God is with us, are assembled to consider the things wherein we agree and the things wherein we differ. We now receive the following series of reports as containing subject matter for the consideration of our respective Churches in their common search for unity.

2   This is a Conference summoned to consider matters of Faith and Order. It is emphatically *not* attempting to define the conditions of future reunion. Its object is to register the apparent level of fundamental agreements within the Conference and the grave points of disagreements remaining; also to suggest certain lines of thought which may in the future tend to a fuller measure of agreement.

3   Each subject on the agenda was first discussed in plenary session. It was then committed to one of the sections, of more than one hundred members each, into which the whole Conference was divided. The report, after full discussion in subsection, was finally drawn up and adopted

unanimously or by a large majority vote by the section to which it had been committed. It was twice presented for further discussion to a plenary session of the Conference when it was referred to the Churches in its present form.

4 Though we recognise the reports to be neither exhaustive nor in all details satisfactory to every member of the Conference, we submit them to the Churches for that deliberate consideration which could not be given in the brief period of our sessions. We thank God and rejoice over agreements reached; upon our agreements we build. Where the reports record differences, we call upon the Christian world to an earnest reconsideration of the conflicting opinions now held, and a strenuous endeavour to reach the truth as it is in God's mind, which should be the foundation of the Church's unity.

I. THE CALL TO UNITY

Unanimously adopted by the full Conference,

5 God wills unity. Our presence in this Conference bears testimony to our desire to bend our wills to His. However we may justify the beginnings of disunion, we lament its continuance and henceforth must labour, in penitence and faith, to build up our broken walls.

6 God's Spirit has been in the midst of us. It was He who called us hither. His presence has been manifest in our worship, our deliberations, and our whole fellowship. He has discovered us to one another. He has enlarged our horizons, quickened our understanding, and enlivened our hope. We have dared and God has justified our daring. We can never be the same again. Our deep thankfulness must find expression in sustained endeavour to share the visions vouchsafed us here with those smaller home groups where our lot is cast.

7 More than half the world is waiting for the Gospel. At home and abroad sad multitudes are turning away in bewilderment from the Church because of its corporate feebleness. Our missions count that as a necessity which we are inclined to look on as a luxury. Already the mission field is impatiently revolting from the divisions of the Western Church to make bold adventure for unity in its own right. We of the Churches represented in this Conference cannot allow our spiritual children to outpace us.

We with them must gird ourselves to the task, the early beginnings of which God has so richly blessed, and labour side by side until our common goal is reached.

8   Some of us, pioneers in this undertaking, have grown old in our search for unity. It is to youth that we look to lift the torch on high. We men have carried it too much alone through many years. The women henceforth should be accorded their share of responsibility. And so the whole Church will be enabled to do that which no section can hope to perform.

It was God's clear call that gathered us. With faith stimulated by His guidance to us here, we move forward.

II. THE CHURCH'S MESSAGE TO THE WORLD— THE GOSPEL

REPORT OF SECTION II

Received by the full Conference, *nemine contradicente*

9   The message of the Church to the world is and must always remain the Gospel of Jesus Christ. The Gospel is the joyful message of redemption, both here and hereafter, the gift of God to sinful man in Jesus Christ.

10   The world was prepared for the coming of Christ through the activities of God's Spirit in all humanity, but especially in His revelation as given in the Old Testament; and in the fulness of time the eternal Word of God became incarnate, and was made man, Jesus Christ, the Son of God and the Son of Man, full of grace and truth.

11   Through His life and teaching, His call to repentance, His proclamation of the coming of the Kingdom of God and of judgment, His suffering and death, His resurrection and exaltation to the right hand of the Father, and by the mission of the Holy Spirit, He has brought to us forgiveness of sins, and has revealed the fulness of the living God and His boundless love toward us. By the appeal of that love, shown in its completeness on the Cross, He summons us to the new life of faith, self-sacrifice, and devotion to His service and the service of men.

12   Jesus Christ, as the crucified and the living One, as Saviour and Lord, is also the centre of the world-wide Gospel of the Apostles and the Church. Because He Himself is the Gospel, the Gospel is the message of the Church

to the world. It is more than a philosophical theory; more than a theological system; more than a programme for material betterment. The Gospel is rather the gift of a new world from God to this old world of sin and death; still more, it is the victory over sin and death, the revelation of eternal life in Him who has knit together the whole family in heaven and on earth in the communion of saints, united in the fellowship of service, of prayer, and of praise.

13   The Gospel is the prophetic call to sinful man to turn to God, the joyful tidings of justification and of sanctification to those who believe in Christ. It is the comfort of those who suffer; to those who are bound it is the assurance of the glorious liberty of the sons of God. The Gospel brings peace and joy to the heart, and produces in men self-denial, readiness for brotherly service, and compassionate love. It offers the supreme goal for the aspirations of youth, strength to the toiler, rest to the weary, and the crown of life to the martyr.

14   The Gospel is the sure source of power for social regeneration. It proclaims the only way by which humanity can escape from those class and race hatreds which devastate society at present into the enjoyment of national well-being and international friendship and peace. It is also a gracious invitation to the non-Christian world, East and West, to enter into the joy of the living Lord.

15   Sympathising with the anguish of our generation, with its longing for intellectual sincerity, social justice and spiritual inspiration, the Church in the eternal Gospel meets the needs and fulfils the God-given aspirations of the modern world. Consequently, as in the past so also in the present, the Gospel is the only way of salvation. Thus, through His Church, the living Christ still says to men "Come unto me! . . . He that followeth me shall not walk in darkness, but shall have the light of life."

III. THE NATURE OF THE CHURCH

REPORT OF SECTION III

Received by the full Conference, *nemine contradicente*

16   God who has given us the Gospel for the salvation of the world has appointed His Church to witness by life and word to its redeeming power. The Church of the Living God is constituted by His own will, not by the will or con-

sent or beliefs of men whether as individuals or as societies, though He uses the will of men as His instrument. Of this Church Jesus Christ is the Head, the Holy Spirit its continuing life.

17   The Church as the communion of believers in Christ Jesus is, according to the New Testament, the people of the New Covenant; the Body of Christ; and the Temple of God, built upon the foundation of the Apostles and Prophets, Jesus Christ Himself being the chief cornerstone.

18   The Church is God's chosen instrument by which Christ, through the Holy Spirit, reconciles men to God through faith, bringing their wills into subjection to His sovereignty, sanctifying them through the means of grace, and uniting them in love and service to be His witnesses and fellow workers in the extension of His rule on earth until His Kingdom come in glory.

19   As there is but one Christ, and one life in Him, and one Holy Spirit who guides into all truth, so there is and can be but one Church, holy, catholic, and apostolic.

20   The Church on earth possesses certain characteristics whereby it can be known of men. These have been, since the days of the Apostles, at least the following:

1. The possession and acknowledgment of the Word of God as given in Holy Scripture and interpreted by the Holy Spirit to the Church and to the individual. (Note A.)

2. The profession of faith in God as He is incarnate and revealed in Christ.

3. The acceptance of Christ's commission to preach the Gospel to every creature.

4. The observance of the Sacraments.

5. A ministry for the pastoral office, the preaching of the Word, and the administration of the Sacraments.

6. A fellowship in prayer, in worship, in all the means of grace, in the pursuit of holiness, and in the service of man.

21   As to the extent and manner in which the Church thus described finds expression in the existing Churches, we differ. Our differences chiefly concern:

1. The nature of the Church visible and the Church invisible, their relation to each other, and the number of those who are included in each. (Note B.)

31

2. The significance of our divisions past and present. (Note C.)

22 Whatever our views on these points, we are convinced that it is the will of Christ that the one life of the one body should be manifest to the world. To commend the Gospel to doubting, sinful, and bewildered men, a united witness is necessary. We therefore urge most earnestly that all Christians, in fulfilment of our Saviour's prayer that His disciples may be one, reconsecrate themselves to God, that by the help of His Spirit the body of Christ may be built up, its members united in faith and love, and existing obstacles to the manifestation of their unity in Christ may be removed; that the world may believe that the Father has sent Him.

23 We join in the prayer that the time may be hastened when in the name of Jesus every knee shall bow and every tongue confess that Jesus Christ is Lord to the glory of God the Father.

Notes

24 (A.) Some hold that this interpretation is given through the tradition of the Church; others through the immediate witness of the Spirit to the heart and conscience of believers; others through both combined.

25 (B.) For instance
1. Some hold that the invisible Church is wholly in heaven; others include in it all true believers on earth, whether contained in any organisation or not.
2. Some hold that the visible expression of the Church was determined by Christ Himself and is therefore unchangeable; others that the one Church under the guidance of the Holy Spirit may express itself in varying forms.
3. Some hold that one or other of the existing Churches is the only true Church; others that the Church as we have described it is to be found in some or all of the existing Communions taken together.
4. Some, while recognising other Christian bodies as Churches, are persuaded that in the providence of God and by the teaching of history a particular form of ministry has been shown to be necessary to the best welfare of the Church; others hold that no one form of organisation is inherently preferable; still others, that no organisation is necessary.

26 (C) One view is that no division of Christendom has ever come to pass without sin. Another view is that the divisions were the inevitable outcome of different gifts of the Spirit and different understandings of the truth. Between these, there is the view of those who look back on the divisions of the past with penitence and sorrow coupled with a lively sense of God's mercy, which in spite of and even through these divisions has advanced His cause in the world.

IV. THE CHURCH'S COMMON CONFESSION OF FAITH

REPORT OF SECTION IV

Received by the full Conference, *nemine contradicente*

27 We members of the Conference on Faith and Order, coming from all parts of the world in the interest of Christian unity, have with deep gratitude to God found ourselves united in common prayer, in God our heavenly Father and His Son Jesus Christ, our Saviour, in the fellowship of the Holy Spirit.

28 Notwithstanding the differences in doctrine among us, we are united in a common Christian Faith which is proclaimed in the Holy Scriptures and is witnessed to and safeguarded in the Ecumenical Creed, commonly called the Nicene, and in the Apostles' Creed, which Faith is continuously confirmed in the spiritual experience of the Church of Christ.

29 We believe that the Holy Spirit in leading the Church into all truth may enable it, while firmly adhering to the witness of these Creeds (our common heritage from the ancient Church), to express the truths of revelation in such other forms as new problems may from time to time demand.

30 Finally, we desire to leave on record our solemn and unanimous testimony that no external and written standards can suffice without an inward and personal experience of union with God in Christ.

Notes

31 1. It must be noted that the Orthodox Eastern Church can accept the Nicene Creed only in its uninterpolated form without the *filioque* clause; and that although the Apostles' Creed has no place in the formularies of this Church, it is in accordance with its teaching.

33

32   2. It must be noted also that some of the Churches represented in this Conference conjoin tradition with the Scriptures, some are explicit in subordinating Creeds to the Scriptures, some attach a primary importance to their particular Confessions, and some make no use of Creeds.

33   3. It is understood that the use of these Creeds will be determined by the competent authority in each Church, and that the several Churches will continue to make use of such special Confessions as they possess.

V. THE MINISTRY OF THE CHURCH
REPORT OF SECTION V

Received by the full Conference, *nemine contradicente*

34   We members of the Conference on Faith and Order are happy to report that we find ourselves in substantial accord in the following five propositions:

1. The ministry is a gift of God through Christ to His Church and is essential to the being and well-being of the Church.

2. The ministry is perpetually authorised and made effective through Christ and His Spirit.

3. The purpose of the ministry is to impart to men the saving and sanctifying benefits of Christ through pastoral service, the preaching of the Gospel, and the administration of the sacraments, to be made effective by faith.

4. The ministry is entrusted with the government and discipline of the Church, in whole or in part.

5. Men gifted for the work of the ministry, called by the Spirit and accepted by the Church, are commissioned through an act of ordination by prayer and the laying on of hands to exercise the function of this ministry.

35   Within the many Christian communions into which in the course of history Christendom has been divided, various forms of ministry have grown up according to the circumstances of the several communions and their beliefs as to the mind of Christ and the guidance of the New Testament. These communions have been, in God's providence, manifestly and abundantly used by the Holy Spirit in His work of enlightening the world, converting sinners, and perfecting saints. But the differences which have arisen in regard to the authority and functions of these various forms of ministry have been and are the occasion of manifold doubts, questions, and misunderstandings.

36   These differences concern the nature of the ministry (whether consisting of one or several orders), the nature of ordination and of the grace conferred thereby, the function and authority of bishops, and the nature of apostolic succession. We believe that the first step toward the overcoming of these difficulties is the frank recognition that they exist, and the clear definition of their nature. We therefore add as an appendix to our Report such a statement, commending it to the thoughtful consideration of the Churches we represent.

37   By these differences the difficulties of intercommunion have been accentuated to the distress and wounding of faithful souls, while in the mission field, where the Church is fulfiling its primary object to preach the Gospel to every creature, the young Churches find the lack of unity a very serious obstacle to the furtherance of the Gospel. Consequently the provision of a ministry acknowledged in every part of the Church as possessing the sanction of the whole Church is an urgent need.

38   There has not been time in this Conference to consider all the points of difference between us in the matter of the ministry with that care and patience which could alone lead to complete agreement. The same observation applies equally to proposals for the constitution of the united Church. Certain suggestions as to possible church organisation have been made, which we transmit to the Churches with the earnest hope that common study of these questions will be continued by the members of the various Churches represented in this Conference.

39   In view of (1) the place which the episcopate, the councils of presbyters, and the congregation of the faithful, respectively, had in the constitution of the early Church, and (2) the fact that episcopal, presbyteral, and congregational systems of government are each today, and have been for centuries, accepted by great communions in Christendom, and (3) the fact that episcopal, presbyteral and congregational systems are each believed by many to be essential to the good order of the Church, we therefore recognise that these several elements must all, under conditions which require further study, have an appropriate place in the order of life of a reunited Church, and that each separate communion, recalling the abundant blessing of God vouchsafed to its ministry in the past, should gladly

35

bring to the common life of the united Church its own spiritual treasures.

40   If the foregoing suggestion be accepted and acted upon, it is essential that the acceptance of any special form of ordination as the regular and orderly method of introduction into the ministry of the Church for the future should not be interpreted to imply the acceptance of any one particular theory of the origin, character, or function of any office in the Church, or to involve the acceptance of any adverse judgment on the validity of ordination in those branches of the Church universal that believe themselves to have retained valid and apostolic Orders under other forms of ordination; or as disowning or discrediting a past or present ministry of the Word and Sacrament which has been used and blessed by the Spirit of God.

41   It is further recognised that inasmuch as the Holy Spirit is bestowed upon every believer, and each believer has an immediate access to God through Jesus Christ, and since special gifts of the Holy Spirit, such as teaching, preaching, and spiritual counsel, are the treasures of the Church as well as of the individual, it is necessary and proper that the Church should make fuller use of such gifts for the development of its corporate spiritual life and for the extension of the Kingdom of Jesus Christ, our Lord.

42   In particular, we share in the conviction, repeatedly expressed in this Conference, that pending the solution of the questions of faith and order in which agreements have not yet been reached, it is possible for us, not simply as individuals but as Churches, to unite in the activities of brotherly service which Christ has committed to His disciples. We therefore commend to our Churches the consideration of the steps which may be immediately practicable to bring our existing unity in service to more effective expression.

43   In conclusion, we express our thankfulness to Almighty God for the great progress which has been made in recent years in the mutual approach of the Churches to one another, and our conviction that we must go forward with faith and courage, confident that with the blessing of God we shall be able to solve the problems that lie before us.

44 1. The following is the view of the Orthodox Church, as formulated for us by its representatives.

"The Orthodox Church, regarding the ministry as instituted in the Church by Christ Himself, and as the body which by a special *charisma* is the organ through which the Church spreads its means of grace such as the sacraments, and believing that the ministry in its threefold form of bishops, presbyters, and deacons can be based only on the unbroken apostolic succession, regrets that it is unable to come in regard to the ministry into some measure of agreement with many of the Churches represented at this Conference; but prays God that He, through His Holy Spirit, will guide to union even in regard to this difficult point of disagreement."

45 2. In western Christendom also there are conspicuous differences.

One representative view includes the following points: (a) that there have always been various grades of the ministry, each with its own function; (b) that ordination is a sacramental act of divine institution, and therefore indispensable, conveying the special *charisma* for the particular ministry; (c) that bishops who have received their office by succession from the Apostles are the necessary ministers of ordination; (d) that the apostolic succession so understood is necessary for the authority of the ministry, the visible unity of the Church, and the validity of the sacraments.

46 On the other hand it is held by many Churches represented in the Conference (a) that essentially there is only one ministry, that of the Word and Sacraments; (b) that the existing ministries in these Churches are agreeable to the New Testament, are proved by their fruits and have due authority in the Church, and the sacraments ministered by them are valid; (c) that no particular form of ministry is necessary to be received as a matter of faith; (d) that the grace which fits men for the ministry is immediately given by God, and is recognised, not conferred, in ordination.

47 Further we record that there are views concerning the ministry which are intermediate between the types just mentioned. For instance, some who adhere to an episcopal

37

system of church government do not consider that the apostolic succession as described above is a vital element of episcopacy, or they reject it altogether. Others do not regard as essential the historic episcopate. Those who adhere to presbyteral systems of church government believe that the apostolic ministry is transmissible and has been transmitted through presbyters orderly associated for the purpose. Those who adhere to the congregational system of government define their ministry as having been and being transmitted according to the precedent and example of the New Testament.

VI. THE SACRAMENTS

REPORT OF SECTION VI

Received by the full Conference, *nemine contradicente*

48   We are convinced that for the purpose in view in this Conference we should not go into detail in considering Sacraments—by some called "Mysteries." The purpose therefore of this statement is to show that there may be a common approach to and appreciation of Sacraments on the part of those who may otherwise differ in conception and interpretation.

49   We testify to the fact that the Christian world gives evidence of an increasing sense of the significance and value of Sacraments, and would express our belief that this movement should be fostered and guided as a means of deepening the life and experience of the Churches. In this connection we recognise that the Sacraments have special reference to the corporate life and fellowship of the Church and that the grace is conveyed by the Holy Spirit, taking of the things of Christ and applying them to the souls through faith.

50   We agree that Sacraments are of divine appointment and that the Church ought thankfully to observe them as divine gifts.

51   We hold that in the Sacraments there is an outward sign and an inward grace, and that the Sacraments are means of grace through which God works invisibly in us. We recognise also that in the gifts of His grace God is not limited by His own Sacraments.

52   The Orthodox Church and others hold that there are seven Sacraments and that for their valid administration there must be a proper form, a proper matter and a proper ministry. Others can regard only Baptism and the Lord's Supper as Sacraments. Others again, while attaching high value to the sacramental principle, do not make use of the outward signs of Sacraments, but hold that all spiritual benefits are given through immediate contact with God through His Spirit. In this Conference we lay stress on the two Sacraments of Baptism and the Lord's Supper, because they are the Sacraments which are generally acknowledged by the members of this Conference.

53   We believe that in Baptism administered with water in the name of the Father, the Son, and the Holy Spirit, for the remission of sins, we are baptised by one Spirit into one body. By this statement it is not meant to ignore the differences in conception, interpretation, and mode which exist among us.

54   We believe that in the Holy Communion our Lord is present, that we have fellowship with God our Father in Jesus Christ His Son, our Living Lord, who is our one Bread, given for the life of the world, sustaining the life of all His people, and that we are in fellowship with all others who are united to Him. We agree that the Sacrament of the Lord's Supper is the Church's most sacred act of worship, in which the Lord's atoning death is commemorated and proclaimed, and that it is a sacrifice of praise and thanksgiving and an act of solemn self-oblation.

55   There are among us divergent views, especially as to (1) the mode and manner of the presence of our Lord; (2) the conception of the commemoration and the sacrifice; (3) the relation of the elements to the grace conveyed; and (4) the relation between the minister of this Sacrament and the validity and efficacy of the rite. We are aware that the reality of the divine presence and gift in this Sacrament cannot be adequately apprehended by human thought or expressed in human language.

56   We close this statement with the prayer that the differences which prevent full communion at the present time may be removed.

2.

EDINBURGH

Second World Conference
on Faith and Order
August 3-18, 1937

FINAL REPORT

II. THE GRACE OF OUR LORD JESUS CHRIST

1   With deep thankfulness to God for the spirit of unity, which by His gracious blessing upon us has guided and controlled all our discussions on this subject, we agree on the following statement and recognise that there is in connection with this subject no ground for maintaining-division between Churches.

(i) The Meaning of Grace

2   When we speak of God's grace, we think of God Himself as revealed in His Son Jesus Christ. The meaning of divine grace is truly known only to those who know that God is Love, and that all that He does is done in love in fulfilment of His righteous purposes. His grace is manifested in our creation, preservation, and all the blessings of this life, but above all in our redemption through the life, death, and resurrection of Jesus Christ, in the sending of the holy and life-giving Spirit, in the fellowship of the Church and in the gift of the Word and Sacraments.

3   Man's salvation and welfare have their source in God alone, who is moved to His gracious activity towards man not by any merit on man's part, but solely by His free, outgoing love.

4   *(ii) Justification and Sanctification*
God in His free outgoing love justifies and sanctifies us through Christ, and His grace thus manifested is appropriated by faith, which itself is the gift of God.

5   Justification and Sanctification are two inseparable aspects of God's gracious action in dealing with sinful man.

6   Justification is the act of God, whereby He forgives our sins and brings us into fellowship with Himself, who in Jesus Christ, and by His death upon the Cross, has condemned sin and manifested His love to sinners, reconciling the world to Himself.

7   Sanctification is the work of God, whereby through the Holy Spirit He continually renews us and the whole Church, delivering us from the power of sin, giving us increase in holiness, and transforming us into the likeness of His Son through participation in His death and in His risen life. This renewal, inspiring us to continual spiritual activity and conflict with evil, remains throughout the gift of God. Whatever our growth in holiness may be, our fellowship with God is always based upon God's forgiving grace.

8   Faith is more than intellectual acceptance of the revelation in Jesus Christ; it is wholehearted trust in God and His promises, and committal of ourselves to Jesus Christ as Saviour and Lord.

(iii) The Sovereignty of God and Man's Response

9   In regard to the relation of God's grace and man's freedom, we all agree simply upon the basis of Holy Scripture and Christian experience that the sovereignty of God is supreme. By the sovereignty of God we mean His all-controlling, all-embracing will and purpose revealed in Jesus Christ for each man and for all mankind. And we wish further to insist that this eternal purpose is the expression of God's own loving and holy nature. Thus we men owe our whole salvation to His gracious will. But, on the other hand, it is the will of God that His grace should be actively appropriated by man's own will and that for such decision man should remain responsible.

10   Many theologians have made attempts on philosophical lines to reconcile the apparent antithesis of God's sovereignty and man's responsibility, but such theories are not part of the Christian Faith.

11   We are glad to report that in this difficult matter we have been able to speak with a united voice, so that we

have found that here there ought to be no ground for maintaining any division between Churches.

(iv) The Church and Grace

12   We agree that the Church is the Body of Christ and the blessed company of all faithful people, whether in heaven or on earth, the communion of saints. It is at once the realisation of God's gracious purposes in creation and redemption, and the continuous organ of God's grace in Christ by the Holy Spirit, who is its pervading life, and who is constantly hallowing all its parts.

13   It is the function of the Church to glorify God in its life and worship, to proclaim the gospel to every creature, and to build up in the fellowship and life of the Spirit all believing people, of every race and nation. To this end God bestows His Grace in the Church on its members through His Word and Sacraments, and in the abiding presence of the Holy Spirit.

(v) Grace, the Word and the Sacraments

14   We agree that the Word and the Sacraments are gifts of God to the Church through Jesus Christ for the salvation of mankind. In both the grace of God in Christ is shown forth, given, and through faith received; and this grace is one and indivisible.

15   The Word is the appointed means by which God's grace is made known to men, calling them to repentance, assuring them of forgiveness, drawing them to obedience and building them up in the fellowship of faith and love.

16   The Sacraments are not to be considered merely in themselves, but always as sacraments of the Church, which is the Body of Christ. They have their significance in the continual working of the Holy Spirit, who is the life of the Church. Through the sacraments God develops in all its members a life of perpetual communion lived within its fellowship, and thus enables them to embody His will in the life of the world; but the loving-kindness of God is not to be conceived as limited by His sacraments.

17   Among or within the Churches represented by us there is a certain difference of emphasis placed upon the Word and the sacraments, but we agree that such a difference need not be a barrier to union.

(vi) Sola Gratia

18   Some Churches set great value on the expression *sola gratia*, while others avoid it. The phrase has been the sub-

ject of much controversy, but we can all join in the following statement: Our salvation is the gift of God and the fruit of His grace. It is not based on the merit of man, but has its root and foundation in the forgiveness which God in His grace grants to the sinner whom He receives to sanctify him. We do not, however, hold that the action of the divine grace overrides human freedom and responsibility; rather, it is only as response is made by faith to divine grace that true freedom is achieved. Resistance to the appeal of God's outgoing love spells, not freedom, but bondage, and perfect freedom is found only in complete conformity with the good and acceptable and perfect will of God.

III. THE CHURCH OF CHRIST AND THE WORD OF GOD

(i) The Word of God

19   We concur in affirming that the Word of God is ever living and dynamic and inseparable from God's activity. "In the beginning was the Word, and the Word was with God, and the Word was God." God reveals Himself to us by what He does, by that activity by which He has wrought the salvation of men and is working for their restoration to personal fellowship with Himself.

20   He calls and fashions His chosen people and speaks His Word to His prophets and apostles, interpreting to them the meaning of His action. In the fulness of time the Word, the Eternal Son of God, is manifested in Christ our Lord, the Incarnate Word, and His redeeming work, that is, in His words and deeds, in His life and character, in His suffering, death, and resurrection, culminating in the gift of the Spirit and in the life which He gives to the Church which is His body.

21   This divine revelation is addressed to man in the wholeness of his personality, and is apprehended by faith.

22   We are at one in asserting the uniqueness and supremacy of the revelation given in Christ, in whose Name alone salvation is offered to the world. But when we turn from this to the question whether we can come to know God through other and partial revelations we find differences which demand further study and discussion. None of us

43

holds that there is a revelation *out*side Christ which can be put on the same level as the revelation *in* Christ. But while some are prepared to recognise a *praeparatio evangelica* not only in Hebrew but also in other religions, and believe that God makes Himself known in nature and in history, others hold that the only revelation which the Church can know and to which it should witness is the revelation in Jesus Christ, as contained in the Old and New Testaments.

(ii) Holy Scripture and Tradition[1]

23   A testimony in *words* is by divine ordering provided for the revelation uttered by the *Word*. This testimony is given in Holy Scripture, which thus affords the primary norm for the Church's teaching, worship, and life. We discern a parallel, though an imperfect one, between the inspiration of Holy Scripture and the incarnation of the Word in Our Lord Jesus Christ: in each there is a union, effected by the Holy Spirit, between the divine and the human, and an acceptance, for God's saving purpose, of human limitations. "We have this treasure in earthen vessels." We are all convinced that this conception of the revelation cannot be shaken by scientific Bible research. But if it is conscious of its true nature, such research can render the Church important services in bringing about a right interpretation of the Scripture, provided that the freedom needed for carrying out its work is not denied to it.

24   Further, there is matter for fuller discussion in the problem of the tradition of the Church and its relation to Holy Scripture. By tradition is meant the living stream of the Church's life. Thus the Orthodox East, but not it alone, allows that there may be widespread opinions which, as being contrary to Scripture, cannot be considered to have the true authority of tradition, but it does not exclude from tradition some beliefs which do not rest explicitly on Scripture, though they are not in contradiction with it.

25   We are at one in recognising that the Church, enlightened by the Holy Spirit, has been instrumental in the formation of the Bible. But some of us hold that this implies that the Church under the guidance of the Spirit is entrusted with the authority to explain, interpret, and complete ($\sigma\upsilon\mu\pi\lambda\eta\rho\upsilon\tilde{\upsilon}\nu$) the teaching of the Bible, and consider the witness of the Church as given in tradition as equally

[1]See also this Report, 130

44

authoritative with the Bible itself. Others, however, believe that the Church, having recognised the Bible as the indispensable record of the revealed Word of God, is bound exclusively by the Bible as the only rule of faith and practice and, while accepting the relative authority of tradition, would consider it authoritative only in so far as it is founded upon the Bible itself.

26   We all agree that the Christian Church is constituted by the eternal Word of God made man in Christ and is always vitalised by his Holy Spirit. On the other hand, the divine task given to the Church is to proclaim and bear witness to this Word throughout the world by its preaching, its worship, and its whole life.

(iii) The Church: Our Common Faith

27   We are at one in confessing belief in the Holy Catholic Church. We acknowledge that through Jesus Christ, particularly through the fact of His resurrection, of the gathering of His disciples round their crucified, risen, and victorious Lord, and of the coming of the Holy Spirit, God's almighty will constituted the Church on earth.

28   The Church is the people of the new covenant, fulfilling and transcending all that Israel under the old covenant foreshadowed. It is the household of God, the family in which the Fatherhood of God and the brotherhood of man is to be realised in the children of His adoption. It is the body of Christ, whose members derive their life and oneness from their one living Head; and thus it is nothing apart from Him, but is in all things dependent upon the power of salvation which God has committed to His Son.

29   The presence of the ascended Lord in the Church, His Body, is effected by the power of the one Spirit, who conveys to the whole fellowship the gifts of the ascended Lord, dividing to every man severally as He will, guides it into all the truth and fills it unto all the fulness of God.

30   We all agree that Christ is present in His Church through the Holy Spirit as Prophet, Priest, and King. As Prophet He reveals the divine will and purpose to the Church; as Priest He ever liveth to make intercession for us, and through the eternal sacrifice once offered for us on Calvary, He continually draws His people to the Most High; and as King He rules His Church and is ever establishing and extending His Kingdom.

31   Christ's presence in the Church has been perpetual

45

from its foundation, and this presence He makes effective and evident in the preaching of the Word, in the faithful administration of the Sacraments, in prayer offered in His name, and through the newness of life whereby He enables the faithful to bear witness to Himself. Even though men often prove faithless, Christ will remain faithful to the promise of His presence, and will so continue till the consummation of all things.

32   In their apprehension of this faith different persons lay a different emphasis on one or another aspect. Some lay greater stress on the perpetual and abiding Presence of Christ in His Body and with His people, while others lay greater stress on the fact that Christ is present only where His word is truly preached and received by faith.

33   A point to be studied is in what degree the Christian depends ultimately for his assurance that he is in vital touch with Christ upon the possession of the ministry and sacraments, upon the Word of God in the Church, upon the inward testimony of the Holy Spirit, or upon all of these.

(iv) The Church: Agreements and Differences

34   The Church, then, is the body of those on whom the call of God rests to witness to the grace and truth of God. This visible body was, before the Lord came, found in Israel and it is found now in the new Israel to which is entrusted the ministry of reconciliation. To this visible body the word "Ecclesia" is normally applied in the New Testament, and to it the calling of God belongs. It is the sphere of redemption. Apart from the Church man cannot normally attain full knowledge of God nor worship Him in truth.

35   Different Churches differ in their use of the term "church." Some would apply the term not only to the visible redeemed and redemptive community, but also to the invisible company of the fully redeemed; for only when the word is used in this sense would it be right to say, *"extra ecclesiam nulla salus."* But the invisible Church is no ideal Platonic community distinct from the visible Church on earth. The invisible Church and the visible Church are inseparably connected though their limits are not exactly coterminous. Others regard the use of the term "church" with reference to this invisible company of true Christians known only to God as misleading and unscriptural. To speak of this invisible body as the true Church conveys the disastrous suggestions that the true Church need not be

46

visible and that the visible Church need not be true. We all, however, recognise that the number of those whom God has brought into newness of life and joy in the Holy Ghost, and who have made personal response to the forgiving love of God, has limits hidden from human vision and known only to God.

36   Different Churches hold different views as to the basis of Church membership. Some would hold that all who have been baptized and have not by deed or word repudiated their heritage belong to the Church and are to be regarded as members. Others would confine membership to those who have made an open profession of faith in Christ and in whose lives some measure of the spirit of Christ may be discerned.

(v) The Church and the Kingdom of God

37   The Gospel of Jesus Christ bears witness to the reality both of the Church and of the Kingdom of God.

38   The Church rejoices in the Kingdom of God as present whenever man obeys the will of God. But the Church always looks with glad expectation to the consummation of the Kingdom in the future, since Christ the King, Who is present and active in the Church through the Holy Spirit, is still to be manifested in glory. The kingdom of God realises itself now in a veiled form, until its full manifestation when God shall be all in all.

39   Agreeing in this faith we are not yet of one mind about (a) the relationship of the Church to the Kingdom, and (b) the extent to which the Kingdom is made known here and now.

40   Some stress the kinship between the Church and the Kingdom, others the distinction between them. Some lay emphasis on the actual presence of the Kingdom within the Church and the continuity of the two, holding that the coming of the Kingdom can be seen in the progress of the Church in this world and the work wrought through believers, or even through all men of good will the world over. Others lay emphasis on the Kingdom that is to come in glory; and others again think of the Kingdom as the ever-increasing reign of the righteousness and the love of God as manifested in Jesus Christ in every realm of life.

41   Again, some hold that the progress of the Kingdom can already be seen in this world; others hold that the Church knows the Kingdom by faith only, since the victory of

Christ is still hidden from the world and is destined to remain hidden until the end of this age.

42　　In some Churches these differing conceptions are felt to be of great moment, and act as a barrier to full intercourse, while in others they form no such obstacle but are held side by side without interfering with complete communion.

(vi) The Function of the Church

43　　The function of the Church is to glorify God in adoration and sacrificial service and to be God's missionary to the world. She is to bear witness to God's redeeming grace in Jesus Christ in her corporate life, to proclaim the good news to every creature and to make disciples of all nations, bringing Christ's commandments to communities as well as to individuals. In relation to those who belong to her fellowship or who are placed under her influence, the function of the Church is through the ministry of the Word and the Sacraments, and through Christian education, to make them into convinced Christians conscious of the reality of salvation. The needs of individual souls call for pastoral care and for a fellowship in the things of the Spirit through which the members provoke one another to good works, and to walk worthily of their calling, by true friendship, mutual help, and consolation, and the exercise of loving discipline. She is to intercede for all her members, especially for those who suffer for their faith, and for all mankind.

44　　The Church must proclaim the righteousness of God as revealed in Jesus Christ and thus encourage and guide her members to promote justice, peace, and goodwill among all men and through the whole extent of life. The Church is thus called to do battle against the powers of evil and to seek the glory of God in all things, looking to the day when His Kingdom shall come in the fulness of its power.

(vii) The Gift of Prophecy and the Ministry of the Word

45　　We are agreed that the presence and inspiration of the Holy Spirit are granted to His chosen instruments today, and especially to those called to be ministers of the Word of God. Not only in the corporate life and the teaching of the Church as a whole, but in each of its members according to his ability and calling, the Holy Spirit has come to dwell. Indeed, all perfect and abiding revelation given to us in Christ our Lord would certainly have perished from the world had there been no inspired men to record it and to preach it in every age. This revelation does not belong only to the past; it is also an ever-present word by which God speaks directly to the listening soul.

46   Moreover, all manifestations of the Spirit are manifestations of God's divine activity. It is here that prophecy finds its place in the Church's corporate life. In Christ all the truth of God's redemptive purpose for men is fully and sufficiently contained, but every age has its own problems and its own difficulties, and it is the work of the Spirit in every age to apply the one truth revealed in Christ to the circumstances of the time. Moreover, as past experience shows, these new applications bring to the Church a new understanding of the truth on which they rest. The Spirit may speak by whomsoever He wills. The call to bear witness to the Gospel and to declare God's will does not come to the ordained ministry alone; the Church greatly needs, and should both expect and welcome, the exercise of gifts of prophecy and teaching by laity, both men and women. When prophetic gifts appear it is for the Church not to quench the spirit or despise prophesyings but to test these prophesyings by their accordance with the abiding truth entrusted to it, and to hold fast that which is good.

(viii) "Una Sancta" and Our Divisions

47   Everything which the New Testament teaches concerning the Church presupposes its essential unity. But we, as we confess our faith in the one Church, are conscious of a profound cleavage between that faith and the conditions of the present time.

48   We acknowledge that all who accept Jesus Christ as Son of God and their Lord and Saviour, and realise their dependence upon God's mercy revealed in Him, have in that fact a supernatural bond of oneness which subsists in spite of divergences in defining the divine mystery of the Lord. We rejoice that this sense of kinship is now drawing Christians nearer to each other, and that in many partial ways a foretaste of full fellowship between severed communions is even now being sought and found.

49   But we believe that the divisions of Christendom in every land are such as to hamper the manifestation of the unity of Christ's body. We deplore this with all our hearts; and we desire the Conference to summon members of the Churches to such penitence that not only their leaders, but

the ordinary men and women who hear their message, may learn that the cause of Christian unity is implicit in God's word, and should be treated by the Christian conscience as an urgent call from God.

IV. THE COMMUNION OF SAINTS

50   Wherefore seeing we also are compassed about with so great a cloud of witnesses, let us lay aside every weight, and the sin which doth so easily beset us, and let us run with patience the race that is set before us, looking unto Jesus the author and finisher of our faith.—Heb. xii, 1-2.

We use the term "communion of saints" as meaning that all who are "in Christ" are knit together in one fellowship through the Holy Spirit. This conception, which is found repeatedly in the Scriptures, occurs as a phrase of the Apostles' Creed, and gives expression to a precious truth for all Christians. With some, the phrase is regarded as synonymous with the Holy Catholic Church. For others, it expresses a quality of the Church which is realised only in so far as its members mutually share all the blessings which God bestows. For others, it is the description of a quality of life in those who are in grace. The communion of saints is not always regarded as co-extensive with the Church. For the Orthodox and certain other Churches and individual believers it means fellowship not only with living and departed Christians but also with the holy angels, and, in a very special sense, with the Blessed Virgin Mary.[2]

51   In this connection the way in which we should understand the words "all generations shall call me blessed" was considered. No agreement was reached, and the subject requires further study.

52   The words "the communion of saints" ($\kappa o \iota \nu \omega \nu \iota \alpha \ \tau \hat{\omega} \nu$ $\dot{\alpha} \gamma \iota \omega \nu$) expressed certain well-defined phases of the Christian Gospel and of the doctrine of the Church.

53   In the New Testament the word "saints" is applied to all the baptized. The term is further applied to the patriarchs, prophets, or martyrs of the Old Covenant and to

[2]These last hold that the mother of our Lord, designated as "Theotokos" (God-bearer), the ever-Virgin, should be venerated as the highest of all saints and angels, and of all creation. In addition to the general recognition of the Communion of Saints, they venerate particular saints who are honoured by the Church, and ask their intercession and that of angels before God.

those who, believing in Christ, laid down their lives for Him before they could receive baptism. In every case, the saints are those who are devoted to God, who yield themselves as instruments to His sovereign will. They are saints, not by virtue of their own merits, but through the forgiving grace and love of God.

54 There are Churches which hold that the communion is not as between individuals as such, but as between those who are being sanctified by God in His Church. Their unity is not merely the sum total of individuals, but it is a spiritual solidarity which has reality only in so far as they are in Christ, and thereby in His Church.

55 There are also those who interpret the word ἁγίων as neuter as well as masculine. For them the phrase means sharing in holy things, i.e. the means of grace. They emphasise right relations to holy things as the principal mark of the holiness of the faithful.

56 There are others who regard the Word of God and the Holy Spirit as the sole source of the communion of saints, and at the same time would emphasise righteousness and holiness of life. They would also stress the sacredness and value of the individual's personality. While doing so, they would guard against the evils resulting from an over-emphasised individualism by insisting on the corporate nature of the fellowship in Christ. Since the term "saints" is almost always in the plural in the Scriptures, so it is believed that there is no true sainthood apart from the saintly community.

57 We are agreed that the communion of saints most certainly involves the mutual sharing of both spiritual and temporal blessings on the part of all living Christians. We believe that this mutual sharing should transcend all racial, political, social, and denominational barriers, in the spirit of Gethsemane and the Cross. Such, for example, is the fellowship of those associated in any truly Christian ecumenical movement. Therein we have experienced a very real, though not complete, communion of saints. Therein we humbly believe we experience the presence and power of the Holy Spirit.

58 Any conception of the communion of saints which is confined to the Church on earth alone is defective. Many further see in the communion of saints an affirmation of the unbroken communion between the living and departed

in Christ. They believe themselves to be in communion with the departed and express this in their worship. They rejoice to think that there is a growing consciousness among Christians of nearness to the redeemed in the unseen world, refusing to believe that death severs the communion of those on earth with those departed.

59   For some, it is sufficient to leave their departed ones with God, being linked with them through Christ. Others regard it as a Christian privilege and duty to pray for the departed. Still others, conscious of the living presence, guardianship and help of the saints, ask their prayers before God.

60   We all agree that we ought to remember with thankfulness those who as followers of Christ witnessed a good confession in their day and generation, thereby winning victories for Christ and His Kingdom.

61   We wish to make it clear that "the communion which the saints have with Christ does not make them in any wise partakers of the substance of His Godhead, or to be equal with Christ in any respect." In no circumstances should the cherishing of this doctrine veil or shadow the sufficient and only mediatorship of Jesus Christ as our Lord and Redeemer. Neither must this honouring of the saints descend to superstition or abuse.

62   A right understanding of the doctrine of the communion of saints will help us to realise more vividly both that we are in this life members one of another, and that

"We are come unto mount Zion, and unto the city of the living God, the heavenly Jerusalem, and to an innumerable company of angels, to the general assembly and church of the firstborn, which are written in heaven, and to God the Judge of all, and to the spirits of just men made perfect, and to Jesus the mediator of the new covenant."—Heb. xii, 22-24.

V. THE CHURCH OF CHRIST:
MINISTRY AND SACRAMENTS

(i) The Authority for the Sacraments

63   1. We are agreed that in all sacramental doctrine and practice the supreme authority is our Lord Jesus Christ Himself.

64   2. All the Churches have based their sacramental doctrine

and order upon their belief that,[3] according to the evidence of the New Testament, the sacraments which they accept were instituted by Christ Himself. We are agreed that Baptism and the Lord's Supper occupied from the beginning a central position in the Church's common life, and take their origin from what was said and done by Jesus during His life on earth. Sacramental teaching and practice, therefore, are rightly founded upon the record of the New Testament.

65 3. The sacraments are Christ's gifts to His Church, which is not a static society but a living and growing organism and communion, guided by the Holy Spirit into all truth.[4]

66 4. The Holy Spirit enables the Church, walking by faith in its risen Lord, to interpret Holy Scripture as expressing the living Word of God to every age, and to exercise a stewardship of its tradition concerning the sacraments.

67 5. All Church tradition regarding the sacraments ought to be controlled and tested by Scripture.[5]

(ii) The Nature of the Sacraments

68 1. The sacraments are given by Christ to the Church as outward and visible signs of His invisible grace. They are not bare symbols, but pledges and seals of grace, and means whereby it is received.

69 2. Grace is bestowed in the sacraments within the fellowship of the Church by the personal action of Christ upon the believer. Faith[6] is therefore a necessary condition for the effectual reception of grace.

70 3. God's gracious action is not limited by His sacraments.[7]

71 4. It is our Lord Jesus Christ who through the Holy

[3]Many preferred the original wording of this clause which ran ". . . have based their sacramental doctrine and order upon the evidence of the New Testament that . . ."

[4]Scholars differ in their views of the passages of Scripture relating to the institution of the sacraments by our Lord. Many of the Conference believe that no one who recognises the ministry and the sacraments as Christ's gifts to His Church should be excluded from a united Church on the ground that he does not stand for one particular view of the historical origin of the holy ordinances and the ecclesiastical offices.

[5]The Orthodox and some others would wish to add: "All the Sacraments can be founded upon Holy Scripture as completed, explained, interpreted, and understood in the Holy Tradition by the guidance of the Holy Spirit residing in the Church.

Anglican members observe: "The Church of England, while recognizing the authority of the Church to decree rites and ceremonies, forbids it to ordain anything contrary to the Scriptures, but limits the necessity of Scriptural sanction to articles of faith in things necessary to salvation."

[6]Baptist delegates desire this clause to run "faith on the part of the recipient is there . . ."

[7]Orthodox delegates and some others desire to exclude from the reference of this proposition cases in which failure to receive the sacraments is due to contempt or culpable negligence, since sacraments are divinely instituted means of grace generally necessary for salvation.

Spirit accomplishes every sacrament, and the action of the minister of the Church is only instrumental.

72   5. The sacraments are celebrated by the minister, not in virtue of any personal right of his own, but as minister of the Church.

73   6. Regarding the obligation of the sacraments and the questions whether and in what way they are to be deemed necessary to salvation there is divergence of doctrine among us. We think that some further mutual understanding and agreement on those points is required as a condition of full union.

(iii) The Number of the Sacraments

74   The Orthodox Church, the (Assyrian) Church of the East, the (Coptic) Egyptian-Orthodox Church, the Syrian Orthodox and Armenian Churches and the Old Catholic Churches, and many individual believers, as well as the Roman Catholic Church, hold that there are seven sacraments, but the Protestant Churches accept only two— Baptism and the Eucharist. The Anglican Church has never strictly defined the number of the sacraments, but gives a pre-eminent position to Baptism and the Lord's Supper as alone "generally necessary to salvation."

75   The Society of Friends and the Salvation Army observe no sacraments in the usual sense of that term. (cf. 139)

76   The number of the sacraments largely depends upon the the definitions of the term "sacraments" as given by various Churches. In most of the Protestant Churches there are such solemn religious acts as correspond more or less closely with some or all of the five other sacraments which are taught by the Roman, Orthodox, Old Catholic, and other Churches. And even though the name "sacrament" be refused, they are nevertheless *instituta Dei utilia,* as the second Helvetic Confession puts it.

77   Most of us agree that the question of the number of the sacraments should not be regarded as an insurmountable dividing line when we strive to attain to a united Church.

78   The divergence between the practice of the Society of Friends and the Salvation Army on the one hand, and that of other Churches on the other, admittedly presents serious difficulties, but we trust that even here the Holy Spirit will show us His will.

(iv) Validity

79　1. We agree that the sacraments practised by any Christian Church which believes itself to be observing what Christ appointed for His Church are means of grace to those who partake of them with faith.

80　2. Confusion has sometimes been introduced by the use of the term "valid" in the two following senses:

(a) It is sometimes used synonymously with "efficacious," so that the term "invalid" would imply that a sacrament has no spiritual value and is not a means of grace.

(b) It is sometimes used to imply that the sacrament has been correctly performed.

81　In so far as Christians find themselves obliged by loyalty to Christ and to His Church to judge that the sacraments practised by other Christians are invalid, or doubtfully valid, they should, in the cause of Christian truth and charity, do all in their power to see that the precise meaning of their judgement, and the grounds on which they are obliged to make it, are clearly understood.

82　Many of us are of the opinion, and desire to record our belief, that, although it is the duty of a Church to secure that sacraments should be performed regularly and canonically, yet no judgment should be pronounced by any Church denying the "validity" of the sacraments performed by any Christian Church which believes itself to be observing what Christ appointed for His Church.

83　A special difficulty in regard to union arises from a great difference in doctrine which must not be underestimated. Those Churches which adhere to the doctrine of the Church from the age of the Great Councils to the Reformation regard it as one of the conditions for the validity of any sacrament except baptism (and in some cases, marriage) that it should be performed by a validly ordained or consecrated minister. Thus to them the validity of Holy Order is one of the indispensable conditions of the validity of other sacraments. On the other hand, some other Christians do not hold ordination to be a sacrament of Christ's institution, yet hold that an ordained minister is the proper minister of the Eucharist. Other Christians again hold that ordination is a sacrament, but do not hold it to be an essential condition of the validity of other sacraments, that they should be ministered by a validly ordained presbyter or bishop.

84   3. We believe that every sacrament should be so ordered that all may recognise in it an act performed on behalf of the universal Church.

85   4. To this end there is need of an ordained ministry recognised by all to act on behalf of the universal Church in the administration of the sacraments.

86   *Note:*—The Orthodox delegates submit the following statement:

Validity. As regards to the validity of sacraments the Orthodox delegates would like to confine themselves only to the following statement: According to the Orthodox doctrine valid sacraments are only those which are (1) administered by a canonically ordained and instituted minister and (2) rightly performed according to the sacramental order of the Church. They regard it therefore as unnecessary to accept any other document on this matter presented by the Conference.

(v) Baptism

87   Baptism is a gift of God's redeeming love to the Church; and, administered with water in the name of the Father, the Son, and the Holy Spirit, is a sign and seal of Christian discipleship in obedience to our Lord's command.[8] It is generally agreed that the united Church will observe the rule that all members of the visible Church are admitted by Baptism.

88   In the course of discussion it appeared that there were further elements of faith and practice in relation to Baptism about which disagreement existed. Since the time available precluded the extended discussion of such points as baptismal regeneration, the admission of unbaptized persons to Holy Communion,[9] and the relation of Confirmation to Baptism, we are unable to express an opinion as to how far they would constitute obstacles to proposals for a united Church.

(vi) The Eucharist

89   We all believe that Christ is truly present in the Eucharist, though as to how that presence is manifested and

[8]Baptist delegates desire to add as follows: as regards the above statement which has been passed by their brethren who practise infant Baptism, the Baptists could accept it as applying to the baptism of believers, i.e. of those who are capable of making a personal confession of faith (cf. 69). They believe that children belong to God and that no rite is needed to assure His grace for them. This statement of the Baptists was accepted also by a representative of the Disciples of Christ on behalf of that body.

[9]For most Churches this is not an open question, since Baptism is regarded as the only and necessary means of admission to the Church.

realised we may differ. Every precise definition of the presence is bound to be a limiting thing, and the attempt to formulate such definitions and to impose them on the Church has itself been the cause of disunity in the past. The important thing is that we should celebrate the Eucharist with the unfailing use of bread and wine, and of prayer, and of the words of institution, and with agreement as to its essential and spiritual meaning.

90   If sacrifice is understood as it was by our Lord and His followers and in the early Church, it includes, not His death only, but the obedience of His earthly ministry, and His risen and ascended life, in which He still does His Father's will and ever liveth to make intercession for us. Such a sacrifice can never be repeated, but is proclaimed and set forth in the eucharistic action of the whole Church when we come to God in Christ at the Eucharist or Lord's Supper. For us, the secret of joining in that sacrifice is both the worship and the service of God; corporate because we are joined to Christ, and in Him to each other (I Cor. 10:17); individual, because each one of us makes the corporate act of self-oblation his own; and not ceremonial only, but also profoundly ethical, because the keynote of all sacrifice and offering is "Lo! I come to do Thy will, O God." We believe also that the Eucharist is a supreme moment of prayer, because the Lord is the celebrant or minister for us at every celebration, and it is in His prayers for God's gifts and for us all that we join. According to the New Testament accounts of the institution, His prayer is itself a giving of thanks; so that the Lord's Supper is both a *verbum visibile* of the divine grace, and the supreme thanksgiving *(eucharistia)* of the people of God. We are throughout in the realm of Spirit. It is through the Holy Spirit that the blessing and the gift are given. The presence, which we do not try to define, is a spiritual presence. We begin from the historical fact of the Incarnation in the power of the Holy Spirit, and we are already moving forward to the complete spiritual reality of the coming of the Lord and the life of the Heavenly City.[10]

[10]Orthodox delegates desire to add the following statement: *Eucharist.*—(a) The Orthodox Church believes and teaches that in the Sacrament of the Holy Eucharist, which is the extension of the only and once offered sacrifice of our Lord, the offered gifts by virtue of the consecration are changed (*metaballontai*) into the very Body and the very Blood of our Lord Jesus Christ, and given to the faithful for the remission of sins and life everlasting.
(b) The Holy Eucharist can be celebrated only by a validly ordained minister. Certain other Churches and delegates would associate themselves with the Orthodox in making a somewhat similar statement.

(vii) Ministry

A

91　I. The ministry was instituted by Jesus Christ, the Head of the Church, "for the perfecting of the Saints . . . the upbuilding of the body of Christ," and is a gift of God to the Church in the service of the Word and sacraments.

92　II. This ministry does not exclude but presupposes the "royal priesthood," to which all Christians are called as the redeemed of Jesus Christ.

93　III. Ordination to the ministry, according to New Testament teaching and the historic practice of the Church, is by prayer and the laying-on of hands.

94　IV. It is essential to a united Church that it should have a ministry universally recognised.

95　It must be acknowledged, however, that even in connection with these statements, different interpretations are to be reckoned with.

96　For example, while all would agree that the ministry owes its origin to Jesus Christ and is God's gift to the Church, there are differences of judgment regarding the sense in which we may say that the ministry was "instituted" by our Lord.

97　Again, those who agree in accepting the lay-on of hands as the form of ordination differ on the meaning to be attached to the rite, or on the question by whom it should be administered.

98　Further fundamental differences of interpretation arise in connection with the doctrine of Apostolic Succession. In Episcopal Churches it has been thought of both as the succession of bishops in the principal sees of Christendom, handing down and preserving the Apostles' doctrine, and as a succession by laying-on of hands. From early times this double succession has been associated with the stewardship of the sacraments, and is regarded by certain Churches as constituting the true and only guarantee of sacramental grace and right doctrine. This view is represented by the statement formulated by the delegates of the Orthodox Church at Lausanne: Lausanne 44.

99　Substantially the same view finds another expression in the following statement offered on behalf of the Old Catholic Church:

"The Old Catholics maintain that Episcopacy is of apostolic origin, and that it belongs to the essence of the

Church. The Church is the bearer of the ministry. The ministers act only by the commission of the Church. The ministry is received, administered, and handed on in the same sense and in the same way as the Apostles handed it down to the Church. The Apostolic Succession means the inseparability of Church and ministry and the continuity of both."

100   Certain other Churches of the East and some Anglicans would wish to be associated with one or other of the above statements. Other Anglicans would interpret the succession in a more general way to mean the transmission from generation to generation of the authority of ministerial oversight over both clergy and laity in the Church, and they regard it as both a symbol and a bond of unity.

101   In communions of the Presbyterian and Reformed tradition the view is held that the true Apostolic Succession is manifested in a succession of ordination by presbyteries duly constituted and exercising episcopal functions, and in the succession of presbyters in charge of parishes, with special emphasis on the true preaching of the Word and the right administration of the Sacraments. Thus the following statement was presented by Presbyterian delegates:

"Presbyterian delegates desire to have it noted that the conception of the ministry held by their Churches is founded on the identity of 'bishops' and 'presbyters' in the New Testament; that ordination is not by individual presbyter, nor by groups of presbyters, but only by 'presbyters orderly associated' in courts exercising episcopal functions; that a presbyterian succession in orders has been maintained unbroken; and that the functions of the diaconate in the New Testament have been performed not only by those named deacons, but also in some measure by the lay eldership, which in addition to a responsible share in the government and discipline of the Church in all its courts, assists in the dispensing of charity, the visitation of the people, and the distribution of the elements at Holy Communion."

102   Other communions, while unaccustomed to use the term "Apostolic Succession," would accept it as meaning essentially, or even exclusively, the maintenance of the Apostles' witness through the true preaching of the gospel, the right administration of the Sacraments, and the perpetuation of the Christian life in the Christian community.

103   In every case Churches treasure the Apostolic Succession in which they believe.

B

104   In its brief consideration of the form which the ministry might take in the united Church of the future, the Conference started from the following formula in the Report of the Lausanne Conference (See La 39).

105   The acceptance of the "historic Episcopate" carries with it the acceptance of the threefold ministry of bishops, presbyters, and deacons. Many would hold that such acceptance does not require any one dogmatic determination of the doctrine concerning the ministry, while for some this would be requisite. But all who value the "historic Episcopate" hold that it should not be interpreted apart from its historical functions.

106   In a united Church the intimate association of the presbyters in council with the bishop, and of the laity with both, in the government of the Church, should be conserved or restored. Thus the Episcopate would be both constitutional and representative of the whole Church.

107   If the ministry of the united Church should sufficiently include characteristic elements from the episcopal, presbyteral, and congregational systems, the present adherents of those systems would have recognised each others' places in the Church of God, all would be able to find a spiritual home in the united Church, and the doctrine of the Apostolic Succession would, upon a common basis of faith, attain to the fulness which belongs to it by referring at once to the Word, to the ministry and the sacraments, and to the life of the Christian community.

108   It should, however, be recognised that there are members of the Conference who are not persuaded that it is God's will that the one spiritual life of the undivided Church should be expressed through any one form of government, but would find place side by side for Churches of differing form of government, and within or beside the more formally organised body would include freer societies like the Friends and the Salvation Army.

109   The foregoing suggestions are put forward in the knowledge that they contain features which at the present stage may be unacceptable to some Churches on both wings of the Movement, but we are confident that, where the will

to unite exists, the Holy Spirit will enable the Churches in the coming years to improve and develop these first tentative suggestions.

110　　We are alike called of God to pray and to labour by every means for the promotion of this common aim, recognising that the future or ultimate form to be assumed by the united Church must depend not only on the experience of the past, but above all, upon the continued direction of the Holy Spirit.

VI. THE CHURCH'S UNITY IN LIFE AND WORSHIP

(i) *Our Premise and Our Goal*

111　　We take as the premise of our findings and our recommendations the already existing and growing spiritual unity, experienced by Christians as love of one another, understanding of one another, and respect for one another. We believe that no visible unity, acceptable to God and to the people of God, can be achieved save on the foundation of this spiritual unity. We believe that our common experience of spiritual unity derives from the fundamental faith that the Church is the body of Christ, and is, therefore, in principle and ideal, one. In trying to envisage the goal of our endeavours, we are not seeking to create something new; rather we are attempting to discover under the guidance of the Holy Spirit the full nature of the Church created by God in Christ.

112　　Our goal is to realise the ideal of the Church as one living body, worshipping and serving God in Christ, as the fulfilment of our Lord's prayers and of our prayers.

(ii) *The Several Conceptions of Church Unity*

(a) CO-OPERATIVE ACTION

113　　The unity which we seek may be conceived as a confederation or alliance of Churches for *co-operative action.*

114　　In all areas where common purposes and tasks exist, such action is already widely possible without violation of conscience. Church "federations" are the most common expressions of such unity, and one of the most hopeful paths to understanding and brotherly relations. We believe federation, so construed, is a promising approach to more complete forms of unity. We do not share the fears, often expressed, that "federation" in this sense will obscure the goal of a fuller unity or postpone its attainment. The experience of many Churches in many lands forbids such fears, since they run counter to the facts.

115 We recognise that federations for co-operative action should not be construed as examples of "federal union." Certain of our members wish to be recorded as believing that "federal union" is not merely the most we can achieve, but also the most that we should desire.

116 We are agreed that co-operative action between Churches unable to achieve intercommunion or to look toward corporate union, and compelled by fidelity to conscience to remain separate bodies with separate loyalties, is not our final goal, since co-operative action in itself fails to manifest to the world the true character of the Church as one community of faith and worship, as well as of service.

(b) Intercommunion

117 A second aspect of Church unity is commonly indicated by the term "*intercommunion.*" This is the fullest expression of a mutual recognition between two or more Churches. Such recognition is also manifested in the exchange of membership and ministrations.

118 We regard sacramental intercommunion as a necessary part of any satisfactory Church unity. Such intercommunion, as between two or more Churches, implies that all concerned are true Churches, or true branches of the one Church.

119 We think that it should be pointed out that the word "intercommunion" has at present several different connotations. In the fullest sense it means a relation between two or more Churches in which the communion of each is open to all members of the other at all times. This is to be distinguished from relations in which the communion of one Church is "open" to members of other Churches without complete reciprocal recognition, and still more from the occasional welcoming of members of other Churches by a Church whose normal rule would exclude them. We believe that "regularity" and "mutuality" belong to the full meaning of intercommunion. When this term "intercommunion" is used in discussion of Church unity, its meaning should be clearly defined.

120 We must note also the occasions on which at a gathering of Christian people united in a common enterprise, a

Church has invited all who have full status in their own Churches to receive the Holy Communion according to the rite of the inviting Church. This has occurred both at Oxford and at Edinburgh during the Conference held this year. It is to be distinguished both from "intercommunion" and "open communion" as usually understood, and from such "joint celebration" as took place at Jerusalem in 1928.

(c) Corporate Union

121   The third form in which the final goal of our movement may be expressed presents, from the standpoint of definition, the greatest difficulties. It is commonly indicated by such terms as "corporate union" or "organic unity."

122   These terms are forbidding to many, as suggesting the ideal of a compact governmental union involving rigid uniformity. We do not so understand them, and none of us desires such uniformity. On the contrary, what we desire is the unity of a living organism, with the diversity characteristic of the members of a healthy body.

123   The idea of "corporate union" must remain for the vast majority of Christians their ideal. In a Church so united the ultimate loyalty of every member would be given to the whole body and not to any part of it. Its members would move freely from one part to another and find every privilege of membership open to them. The sacraments would be the sacraments of the whole body. The ministry would be accepted by all as a ministry of the whole body.

124   Our task is to find in God, to receive from God as His gift, a unity which can take up and preserve in one beloved community all the varied spiritual gifts which He has given us in our separations. Such a living community, like all that lives, cannot be a construction; life can come only from life; the visible unity of the Body of Christ can issue only from the Living God through the work of the life-giving Spirit.

125   While we do not conceive of the "corporate union," which we seek from God, as a rigid governmental unity, we find it difficult to imagine that unity, as it would exist between Churches within the same territory, without some measure of organisational union. At the same time, we can hardly imagine a corporate union which should provide for the relative autonomy of the several constituent parts in entire neglect of the "federal" principle.

126   In particular, and with immediate reference to the existing world situation, we do not believe that a Church, "corporately" united, could be an effective international community without some permanent organ of conference and counsel, whatever might be the authority and powers of that organ.

(iii) *The Forms of Likeness Basic for Church Unity*

127   1. LIKENESS IN FAITH OR CONFESSION AS A BASIS FOR UNITY. (a)[11] Likeness in faith or confession is not necessary for co-operative action, but we find that essential unity in faith or confession is a necessary basis for (b) full intercommunion and for (c) corporate union.

Such essential unity in faith would be sufficiently expressed for many of the Churches represented in this Conference by such a statement as the following:

We accept as the supreme standard of the faith the revelation of God contained in the Holy Scriptures of the Old and New Testaments and summed up in Jesus Christ.

We acknowledge the Apostles' Creed and the Creed commonly called the Nicene, as witnessing to and safeguarding that faith, which is continuously verified in the spiritual experience of the Church and its members—remembering that these documents are sacred symbols and witnesses of the Christian faith rather than legalistic standards.

We further affirm that the guidance of God's Holy Spirit did not cease with the closing of the canon of the Scripture, or with the formulation of the creeds cited, but that there has been in the Church through the centuries, and still is, a divinely sustained consciousness of the presence of the living Christ. (*Note:* Known in the Orthodox Church as the Holy Tradition.)

Finally, we are persuaded, in the classical words of one of the non-confessional communions, that "God has yet more light to break forth from His Holy Word" for humble and waiting Church. We Christians of this present age should therefore seek the continued guidance of the Spirit of the living God, as we confront our troubled time.

[11]These letters in subsection (iii) refer to the three headings in subsection (ii) above.

128   Some of the Churches represented in the Conference hold that Scripture is not only the supreme but the sole standard and source of Christian faith; they reject any suggestion of the equivalence of Scripture and tradition and any implication that the ancient creeds contain a sufficient interpretation of the Scriptural faith. Some of these Churches regard certain later confessions as possessing an importance and authority at least equal to that of the ancient creeds.[12]

129   The Orthodox and certain other Churches can accept the Nicene Creed only in its uninterpolated form without the *filioque* clause, and those Churches and others hold that the "Holy Tradition" must be acknowledged as a standard and source of the faith complementary to, though wholly consonant with, the revelation in Scripture.

2. LIKENESS IN NON-SACRAMENTAL WORSHIP.

130   (a) Likeness in non-sacramental worship is not necessary for co-operative action.

131   (c) In the non-sacramental worship of God the Father, Son and Holy Spirit, we are agreed that there is little remaining occasion for maintaining the existing divisions between our Churches, and much common ground already exists for further unity.

132   We are all united, in such worship, in the use of the Holy Scriptures. We are further united in common prayer, which may be expressed in the spoken word, through silence, or by employment of the sacred treasures of Christian literature, art, and music. In this worship we all stand before God in adoration of His Majesty, bringing to Him our own needs and the needs of our fellows. We wait for His grace in the forgiveness of our sins and for the restoration of our spirits through renewed communion with Him, and we dedicate ourselves to His service and the service of all mankind.

3. LIKENESS IN SACRAMENTAL FAITH AND PRACTICE.

133   (a) Co-operative activities do not require likeness in doctrine and administration of the sacraments.

134   (b) For Intercommunion.

        (i) Some of us hold that Churches which within their own order practise the two Gospel sacraments can freely

[12]See also this Report 23-26 and La 33

allow intercommunion between their respective members.

(ii) Others hold that no such intercommunion can take place until their Churches have agreed as to the validity of each other's ministrations of these, to them, essential sacraments.

135   (c) For full corporate union it will be necessary to reconcile the differences between Churches which insist, some upon two sacraments, some upon seven, and some upon no formal sacraments whatsoever.

136   The sacrament of the Lord's Supper (or Eucharist) is the Church's most sacred act of worship. Unity in sacramental worship requires essential unity in sacramental faith and practice.

137   The Society of Friends, in the silence of its meetings, seeks without formal sacraments the Real Presence of Him who suffered death that mankind might have life (cf. 75).

138   In this connection we find much cause for encouragement in (i) the liturgical movement on the Continent, and among the non-liturgical Churches in many other lands, and (ii) the increasing opportunities allowed for silence, and for spontaneity among those who use traditional liturgies. In this matter the distinction between liturgical and non-liturgical forms of worship is a diminishing occasion for division.

4. Likeness of Orders as a Basis for Unity.

139   (a) Lack of likeness of orders is no obstacle to co-operative action.

140   For (b) full intercommunion and (c) corporate union it will be necessary to reconcile the differences between Churches which hold (i) that a ministry in the threefold form of bishops, priests, and deacons was instituted in the Church by Christ; (ii) that the historic episcopate is essential for corporate union; (iii) that a ministry was instituted by Christ in which bishops as distinct from presbyters are not essential; (iv) that no specially ordained ministry whatsoever is required by the conception of the Church.

5. Likeness in Polity as a Basis for Unity.

141   (a) Likeness in polity is not necessary for co-operative action.

142　(c) With reference to corporate union most of us endorse the following statement from the Lausanne Report (see La 39).

143　It will be noted that the above statements assume a substantial likeness, already existing or conceded in theory with respect to faith, confession, worship, polity.

144　It will be further noted that there is a marked unlikeness, whether as a matter of existing practice or as a matter of rival doctrines, when we are considering sacraments and orders.

(iv) *Obstacles to Church Unity*

1. OBSTACLES WHICH ARE RESTRICTED TO "FAITH" AND "ORDER"

145　We find that the obstacles most difficult to overcome consist of elements of "faith" and "order" combined, as when some form of Church government or worship is considered a part of the faith.

146　But we are led to the conclusion that behind all particular statements of the problem of corporate union lie deeply divergent conceptions of the Church. For the want of any more accurate terms this divergence might be described as the contrast between "authoritarian" and "personal" types of Church.

147　We have, on the one hand, an insistence upon a divine givenness in the Scriptures, in orders, in creeds, in worship.

148　We have, on the other hand, an equally strong insistence upon the individual experience of divine grace, as the ruling principle of the "gathered" Church, in which freedom is both enjoyed as a religious right and enjoined as a religious duty.

149　We are aware that between these extremes many variations exist, expressed as well in doctrine as in organisation, worship, and types of piety. These variations are combinations of the two contrasted types of Church to which we have referred.

150　We do not minimise the difficulties which these contrasted types of Church present to our movement, nor are we willing to construe them as being due mainly to misunderstandings or to sin.

151　It is our hope and prayer that through the guidance

of the Holy Spirit they may, in God's good time, be overcome.

152   Meanwhile it is our duty to attempt by study to enter still more sympathetically into the experience of others, and to "keep the unity of the Spirit in the bond of peace."

153   We suggest that the full range of the contrast between the two types of Church to which we have been referring, is in no wise covered by the antithesis of episcopal and non-episcopal orders.

154   This contrast may be expressed in many other terms. The problem of the authority of Scripture and the modes of its interpretation is the most classical instance,

2. Obstacles not restricted to "Faith" and "Order"

155   (a) Obstacles which are, in part, theological or ecclesiastical, and, in equal part, sociological or political.

Such obstacles are met in the case of a national Church which hallows the common life of a given people, but is at the same time exposed to the perils of an exclusive provincialism or of domination by a secular state.

Frequently renewed testimony, given at this Conference, makes it plain that the Churches of the mission field are grievously hindered in their efforts to solve problems of this order so long as they remain unsolved in the "home" lands.

156   (b) Obstacles which are due mainly to historical factors.

We have, in Western Christendom, many separations which are the result of the divided secular history of Europe.

We have, in the Near and Middle East, certain conspicuous examples of religiously isolated communities, whose isolation is primarily due to their loyalty to an ancient heritage which goes back to earliest Christian times and often to lands far off from those in which they now exist.

157   (c) Obstacles which are of "cultural" origin.

In Churches which already enjoy substantial agreement upon matters of faith and order, and which may be said to stand upon common ground as representatives of one or other of the two contrasted types of Church, the prospect of corporate union is by no means clear or assured.

These Churches are not conscious of any obstacles to such union because of mutually exclusive doctrines. They are, however, kept apart by barriers of nationality, race, class, general culture, and, more particularly, by slothful self-content and self-sufficiency.

(v) *What Can We Do to Move Toward the Unity We Seek?*

158 The unity we seek is not simple but complex. It has two aspects: (a) the inner spiritual unity known in its completeness to God alone; and (b) the outward unity which expresses itself in mutual recognition, co-operative action and corporate or institutional unity. The concrete proposals here brought forward may be regarded as next steps toward the realisation of the unity which the Churches should seek. Some of these proposals are of concern to individual communions, others of concern to groups of communions in certain countries or other areas, and still others may be considered as of ecumenical or worldwide range.

(159-166)

5. SPECIAL TIMES OF PRAYER.

167 The practice in some countries of setting apart one Sunday each year for special prayer for the oecumenical movement is worthy of wide observance. Since 1920 the worldwide observance of the eight days before Pentecost (Whitsunday) as a special time of prayer for the unity of Christ's Church has been fostered by the Faith and Order Movement. . . .

(168-170)

8. PRINCIPLES OF CO-OPERATION.

171 It is widely recognised that sound policies of co-operation in all spheres of Christian action have done much to facilitate the drawing together of the Christian Churches. Such co-operation between Christian bodies, if it is to be truly effective, must have regard to certain guiding principles and governing considerations drawn from experience already accumulated in many countries.

172 Among these attention is called to the following:

(1) In determining the sphere of co-operation due regard is paid to the objects to be achieved, namely:

(a) to meet real and recognised need;

69

(b) to obviate conflict and unnecessary waste;

(c) to accomplish important results which cannot be secured as well, if at all, by the co-operative agencies working separately.

(2) At the very beginning of the undertaking the various bodies joining in the co-operative arrangement enter into an understanding as to objectives, scope, direction, assignment of responsibilities, support, and all else vital to the success of the undertaking, and this understanding is set forth with clarity in writing.

(3) The co-operative agency possesses only such power as the co-operating bodies confer upon it.

(4) The plan of organisation is made as simple as is compatible with achieving the desired results.

(5) Everything is done openly and in consultation.

(6) There is a sincere determination to understand the viewpoints and the distinctive characteristics of the different units, and willingness to accept what others have to give.

(7) Wherever co-operation is undertaken, it is carried through so thoroughly as to create the confidence on which further developments must depend.

(8) No large venture of co-operation can proceed to high success without adequate financial resources, but it is believed that those will be forthcoming if the other conditions here emphasised are met.

(9) The leaders are on their guard lest in their own lives there be manifested or tolerated those things which tend to destroy co-operation or to make impossible true Christian unity; for example, ignorance and prejudice, hazy thinking and vague statements, selfish ambition and jealousy, suspicion and lack of frankness, intriguing and disloyalty.

(10) The prime consideration to be borne constantly in mind by all engaged in the work of co-operation is that of rendering Christlike service. First and last in point of importance is the recognition of the Lordship of Jesus Christ, and the conviction that He Himself wills co-operation and unity.

13. PLANS FOR CHURCH UNION.

180   It is recommended that communions represented at the present Conference should consider the desirability of setting up effective standing commissions for the study of the oecumenical questions, for fostering mutually helpful relations with other communions, and for conducting conversations with other communions leading toward Church union.

181   It is highly desirable, in countries where conditions are favorable and the time seems ripe, that those communions which already enjoy a considerable measure of mutual understanding, fellowship, and co-operation should proceed without undue delay to the stage of official negotiations, or at least of conversations, and in particular should produce, as soon as may be, a preliminary or provisional draft scheme of union for submission to their constituencies.

182

15. TERRITORIAL AND ECUMENICAL UNITY.

183   A problem calling for far-sighted policy is that presented in areas where, when union is under discussion, it becomes necessary for a Church to choose between, on the one hand, entering into a unity with other denominations within the same national boundary, and, on the other hand, maintaining connections with other Churches of its own order throughout the world. Experience shows that the injury done to the Christian cause by the multiplicity of separate Churches within a given area is so great that the territorial unity of Churches should normally be regarded as desirable where it can be accomplished without violating the principles of the Churches concerned. It must, however, be recognised that the ideal of a territorially or nationally united Church is accompanied by certain dangers. Therefore we urge that in developing Church union on the territorial basis every care should be taken to preserve in nationally constituted Churches a sense of oecumenical relationship, and to maintain such relationship in every possible way. . . .

17. THE COUNCIL OF CHURCHES.

186   This Conference as well as the World Conference held at Oxford have approved in principle the proposal that the Churches should form a Council of Churches. Some members of this Conference desire to place on record their opposition to this proposal, but we are agreed that if the Churches should adopt it, the Council should be so designed as to conserve the distinctive character and value of each of the movements represented in the two Conferences. To this end it is desirable that, while freedom should be exercised in the formation of special committees, the Churches as such should come together on the basis of the doctrine of the Incarnation. The largest success of the plan depends upon securing adequate representation of every communion.

AFFIRMATION OF UNION IN ALLEGIANCE TO OUR LORD JESUS CHRIST

187   The Second World Conference on Faith and Order, held in Edinburgh in August, 1937, brought together four hundred and fourteen delegates from one hundred and twenty-two Christian communions in forty-three different countries. The delegates assembled to discuss together the causes that keep Christian communions apart, and the things that unite them in Christian fellowship. The Conference approved the following statement *nemine contradicente:*

188   We are one in faith in our Lord Jesus Christ, the incarnate Word of God. We are one in allegiance to Him as Head of the Church, and as King of kings and Lord of lords. We are one in acknowledging that this allegiance takes precedence of any other allegiance that may make claims upon us.

189   This unity does not consist in the agreement of our minds or the consent of our wills. It is found in Jesus Christ Himself, Who lived, died, and rose again to bring us to the Father, and Who through the Holy Spirit dwells in His Church. We are one because we are all the objects of the love and grace of God, and called by Him to witness in all the world to His glorious gospel.

190   Our unity is of heart and spirit. We are divided in the outward forms of our life in Christ, because we understand differently His will for His Church. We believe, however, that a deeper understanding will lead us toward a united apprehension of the truth as it is in Jesus.

191   We humbly acknowledge that our divisions are contrary to the will of Christ, and we pray God in His mercy to shorten the days of our separation and to guide us by His Spirit into fulness of unity.

192   We are thankful that during recent years we have been drawn together; prejudices have been overcome, misunderstandings removed, and real, if limited, progress has been made toward our goal of a common mind.

193   In this Conference we may gratefully claim that the Spirit of God has made us willing to learn from one another, and has given us a fuller vision of the truth and enriched our spiritual experience.

194   We have lifted up our hearts together in prayer; we have sung the same hymns; together we have read the same Holy Scriptures. We recognise in one another, across the barriers of our separation, a common Christian outlook and a common standard of values. We are therefore assured of a unity deeper than our divisions.

195   We are convinced that our unity of spirit and aim must be embodied in a way that will make it manifest to the world, though we do not yet clearly see what outward form it should take.

196   We believe that every sincere attempt to co-operate in the concerns of the kingdom of God draws the severed communions together in increased mutual understanding and goodwill. We call upon our fellow Christians of all communions to practise such co-operation; to consider patiently occasions of disunion that they may be overcome; to be ready to learn from those who differ from them; to seek to remove those obstacles to the furtherance of the gospel in the non-Christian world which arise from our divisions; and constantly to pray for that unity which we believe to be our Lord's will for His Church.

197   We desire also to declare to all men everywhere our assurance that Christ is the one hope of unity for the world in face of the distractions and dissensions of this present time. We know that our witness is weakened by our

divisions. Yet we are one in Christ and in the fellowship of His Spirit. We pray that everywhere, in a world divided and perplexed, men may turn to Jesus Christ our Lord, Who makes us one in spite of our divisions; that He may bind in one those who by many worldly claims are set at variance; and that the world may at last find peace and unity in Him; to Whom be glory for ever.

3.

AMSTERDAM

First Assembly of
the World Council of Churches
August 22—September 4, 1948

I. THE MESSAGE OF THE ASSEMBLY

1 . . . We bless God our Father, and our Lord Jesus Christ, Who gathers together in one the children of God that are scattered abroad. He has brought us here together at Amsterdam. We are one in acknowledging Him as our God and Saviour. We are divided from one another not only in matters of faith, order, and tradition, but also by pride of nation, class, and race. But Christ has made us His own, and He is not divided. In seeking Him we find one another. Here at Amsterdam we have committed ourselves afresh to Him, and have covenanted with one another in constituting this World Council of Churches. We intend to stay together. We call upon Christian congregations everywhere to endorse and fulfil this covenant in their relations one with another. In thankfulness to God we commit the future to Him. . . .

II. THE UNIVERSAL CHURCH IN GOD'S DESIGN
REPORT OF SECTION I

Received by the Assembly and commended to the churches for their serious consideration and appropriate action.

1. *Our Given Unity*

2   God has given to His people in Jesus Christ a unity which is His creation and not our achievement. We praise and thank Him for a mighty work of His Holy Spirit, by which we have been drawn together to discover that, notwithstanding our divisions, we are one in Jesus Christ.

3   We speak, as Christians from many lands and many traditions, first of all to thank God for His goodness. We come from Christian churches which have for long misunderstood, ignored, and misrepresented one another; we come from lands which have often been in strife; we are all sinful men and we are heirs to the sins of our fathers. We do not deserve the blessing which God has given us.

4   God's redeeming activity in the world has been carried out through His calling a People to be His own chosen People. The Old Covenant was fulfilled in the New when Jesus Christ, the Son of God incarnate, died and was raised from the dead, ascended into heaven and gave the Holy Ghost to dwell in His Body the Church. It is our common concern for that Church which draws us together, and in that concern we discover our unity in relation to her Lord and Head.

2. *Our Deepest Difference*

5   It is in the light of that unity that we can face our deepest difference, still loving one another in Christ and walking by faith in Him alone. It has many forms and deep roots. It exists among many other differences of emphasis within Christendom. Some are Catholic or Orthodox in clearly understood senses; some are Protestant after the great Reformation confessions; others stress the local congregation, the "gathered community" and the idea of the "free church." Some are deeply convinced that Catholic and Protestant (or Evangelical) can be held together within a single church. Yet, from among these shades of meaning, we would draw special attention to a difference to which, by many paths, we are constantly brought back. Historically it has been loosely described as the difference between "Catholic" and "Protestant,"[1] though we have learned to mistrust any oversimple formula to describe it.

6   The essence of our situation is that, from each side of the division, we see the Christian faith and life as a self-

[1] Clearly "Catholic" is not used here to mean Roman Catholic, and "Protestant" in most of Europe is better rendered by "Evangelical."

consistent whole, but our two conceptions of the whole are inconsistent with each other.

7   It is impossible to describe either tendency or emphasis briefly without doing it an injustice. Each contains within it a wide variety of emphasis and many "schools of thought." But in each case we confront a whole corporate tradition of the understanding of Christian faith and life. We may illustrate this by saying that the emphasis usually called "catholic" contains a primary insistence upon the visible continuity of the Church in the apostolic succession of the episcopate. The one usually called "Protestant" primarily emphasizes the initiative of the Word of God and the response of faith, focussed in the doctrine of justification *sola fide*. But the first group also stresses faith and the second also stresses continuity of the visible church in some form. Moreover this difference of emphasis cuts across many of our confessional boundaries. Conversation and understanding between these traditions are often made even more difficult by the presence in each of many who are accustomed only to their own forms of expression, are ignorant of others' traditions and often hold beliefs about their separated fellow Christians which are a travesty of the true situation. Yet even when the conversation is between those who deeply trust and understand each other, there remains a hard core of disagreement between different total ways of apprehending the Church of Christ.

8   Each of these views sees every part of the Church's life in the setting of the whole, so that even where the parts seem to be similar they are set in a context which, as yet, we find irreconcilable with the whole context of the other. As so often in the past, we have not been able to present to each other the *wholeness* of our belief in ways that are mutually acceptable.

3. *Common Beliefs and Common Problems*

9   It is not possible to mention all the points which have been raised in our discussion together, still less to mention those which have been discovered in other fields of work on Christian unity, especially the work of the Commission of "Faith and Order." All that we do here is to indicate certain points to which we have given attention, and some of the ways in which we believe they can be pursued in the work for Christian unity.

77

10   We group our agreements into those which concern the *nature* of the Church and those which concern its *mission*, each followed by some disagreements which are revealed by a closer examination of the agreements.

11   A. We all believe that the Church is God's gift to men for the salvation of the world; that the saving acts of God in Jesus Christ brought the Church into being; that the Church persists in continuity throughout history through the presence and the power of the Holy Spirit.

12   Within this agreement, we should continue, in obedience to God, to try to come to a deeper understanding of our differences in order that they may be overcome. These concern:

13   1. The relation between the old and new Israel and the relation of the visible church to "the new creation" in Christ. It appears from our discussion that some of our differences concerning the Church and the ministry have their roots here.

14   2. The relation, in the saving acts of God in Christ, between objective redemption and personal salvation, between scripture and tradition, between the Church as once founded and the Church as Christ's contemporary act.

15   3. The place of the ministry in the Church and the nature of its authority and continuity, the number and interpretation of the sacraments, the relation of baptism to faith and confirmation, the relation of the universal to the local church; the nature of visible unity and the meaning of schism.

16   B. We believe that the Church has a vocation to worship God in His Holiness, to proclaim the Gospel to every creature. She is equipped by God with the various gifts of the Spirit for the building up of the Body of Christ. She has been set apart in holiness to live for the service of all mankind, in faith and love, by the power of the crucified and risen Lord and according to His example. She is composed of forgiven sinners yet partaking already, by faith, in the eternity of the Kingdom of God and waiting for the consummation when Christ shall come again in the fulness of His glory and power.

17   Within this agreement also we should continue, in obedience to God, to try to come to a deeper understand-

78

ing of our differences in order that they may be overcome. These concern:

18   1. The relation between the Godward vocation of the Church in worship and her manward vocation in witness and service.

19   2. The degree to which the Kingdom of God can be said to be already realised within the Church.

20   3. The nature of the Church's responsibility for the common life of men and their temporal institutions.

21   We gratefully acknowledge these agreements and we seek the solution of these disagreements. God wills the unity of His Church and we must be obedient to Him.

22   At many of these points, our problems cut across confessional boundaries, and we are grateful to God for the way in which we continually learn from our fellow Christians and for the way in which He is making Himself more clearly known to us through our fellowship with one another. In some parts of the world and to some of our members, issues which we have discussed here do not seem important or even relevant. Yet, because they are vital to some, they ultimately concern all. Among others whom we represent, many of our difficulties seem either to have been overcome or are on the way to solution. We thank God for all that lights the path to visible unity.

4. *The Unity in Our Difference*

23   Although we cannot fully meet, our Lord will not allow us to turn away from one another. We cannot ignore one another, for the very intensity of our difference testifies to a common conviction which we drew from Him. The Body of Christ *is* a unity which makes it impossible for us either to forget each other or to be content with agreement upon isolated parts of our belief whilst we leave the other parts unreconciled.

24   Yet we have found God, in His mercy, penetrating the barriers of our fundamental division and enabling us to speak, in the common language of the divine revelation witnessed to in the Scriptures, about the points at which we find we meet. Wherever we find ourselves thus speaking together of our unity, we also find ourselves faced by some stubborn problems. In dealing with them, we discover disagreements which are to be traced back into our dif-

ferent ways of understanding the whole and, beneath those disagreements, we find again an agreement in a unity which drew us together and will not let us go.

5. *The Glory of the Church and the Shame of the Churches*

25   The glory of the Church is wholly in her Lord. In His love, He stooped to redeem her and to crown her as His bride. We praise God for continually renewed signs of His love for the Church. In recent years, it has been given to many of our fellow Christians to rediscover what it is to be a "Church under the Cross." There they discovered new life, found the Bible as a living, contemporary book, made a good confession of their faith and saw the Church come to life in the steadfastness of thousands of humble Christians. We praise God for many signs of awakened life in the churches in many lands. Christ is moving many to a more sacrificial identification with the homeless and desperate, to a more vigorous evangelism, and to a deeper theological seriousness. In many parts of the world, He is drawing long-separate Christians toward a closer approach to unity. Some notable unions have been achieved. For the courage, enterprise, and vision which inspired them, we give thanks to our one Shepherd.

26   Although genuine convictions and loyalty to truth itself have their part in the making and perpetuating of divisions, we confess that pride, self-will and lovelessness have also played their part and still do so.

27   Within our divided churches, there is much which we confess with penitence before the Lord of the Church, for it is in our estrangement from Him that all our sin has its origin. It is because of this that the evils of the world have so deeply penetrated our churches, so that amongst us too there are worldly standards of success, class division, economic rivalry, a secular mind. Even where there are no differences of theology, language, or liturgy, there exists churches segregated by race and colour, a scandal within the Body of Christ. We are in danger of being salt that has lost its savour and is fit for nothing.

28   Within our divided churches it is to our shame that we have so often lived in preoccupation with our internal affairs, looking inward upon our own concerns instead of forgetting ourselves in outgoing love and service. Our churches are too much dominated by ecclesiastic official-

dom, clerical or lay, instead of giving vigorous expression to the full rights of the living congregation and the sharing of clergy and people in the common life in the Body of Christ.

29   We pray for the churches' renewal as we pray for their unity. As Christ purifies us by His Spirit, we shall find that we are drawn together and that there is no gain in unity unless it is unity in truth and holiness.

6. The World Council of Churches

30   We thank God for the ecumenical movement because we believe it is a movement in the direction which He wills. It has helped us to recognise our unity in Christ. We acknowledge that He is powerfully at work amongst us to lead us further to goals which we but dimly discern. We do not fully understand some of the things He has already done amongst us or their implications for our familiar ways. It is not always easy to reconcile our confessional and ecumenical loyalties. We also have much to gain from the encounter of the old-established Christian traditions with the vigorous, growing churches whose own traditions are still being formed. We bring these, and all other difficulties between us into the World Council of Churches in order that we may steadily face them together. Because it is a Council of Churches, we must discuss them in a full sense of responsibility to those who send us, not pretending to agreements which our churches as a whole would repudiate.

31   The World Council of Churches has come into existence because we have already recognised a responsibility to one another's churches in our Lord Jesus Christ. There is but one Lord and one Body. Therefore we cannot rest content with our present divisions. Before God, we are responsible for one another. We see already what some of our responsibilities are, and God will show us more. But we embark upon our work in the World Council of Churches in penitence for what we are, in hope for what we shall be. At this inaugural Assembly, we ask for the continual prayer of all participating churches that God may guide it in His wisdom, saving us both from false claims and from faithless timidity.

81

III. THE CHURCH'S WITNESS TO GOD'S DESIGN
REPORT OF SECTION II

Received unanimously by the Assembly and commended to the churches for their serious consideration and appropriate action

1. *The Purpose of God*

32   The purpose of God is to reconcile all men to Himself and to one another in Jesus Christ His Son. That purpose was made manifest in Jesus Christ—His incarnation, His ministry of service, His death on the Cross, His resurrection and ascension. It continues in the gift of the Holy Spirit, in the command to make disciples of all nations, and in the abiding presence of Christ with His Church. It looks forward to its consummation in the gathering together of all things in Christ. Much in that purpose is still hidden from us. Three things are perfectly plain:

> All that we need to know concerning God's purpose is already revealed in Christ.
>
> It is God's will that the Gospel should be proclaimed to all men everywhere.
>
> God is pleased to use human obedience in the fulfilment of His purpose.

33   To the Church, then, is given the privilege of so making Christ known to men that each is confronted with the necessity of a personal decision, Yes or No. The Gospel is the expression both of God's love to man, and of His claim to man's obedience. In this lies the solemnity of the decision. Those who obey are delivered from the power of the world in which sin reigns, and already, in the fellowship of the children of God, have the experience of eternal life. Those who reject the love of God remain under His judgment and are in danger of sharing in the impending doom of the world that is passing away.

IV. THE CHRISTIAN APPROACH TO THE JEWS
REPORT OF COMMITTEE IV

1. *The Church's commission to preach the Gospel to all men*

34   All of our churches stand under the commission of our common Lord, "Go ye into all the world and preach the

Gospel to every creature." The fulfilment of this commission requires that we include the Jewish people in our evangelistic task.

2. *The special meaning of the Jewish people for Christian faith*

35   In the design of God, Israel has a unique position. It was Israel with whom God made His covenant by the call of Abraham. It was Israel to whom God revealed His name and gave His law. It was to Israel that He sent His Prophets with their message of judgment and of grace. It was Israel to whom He promised the coming of His Messiah. By the history of Israel, God prepared the manger in which in the fulness of time He put the Redeemer of all mankind, Jesus Christ. The Church has received this spiritual heritage from Israel and is therefore in honour bound to render it back in the light of the Cross. We have, therefore, in humble conviction to proclaim to the Jews, "The Messiah for Whom you wait has come." The promise has been fulfilled by the coming of Jesus Christ.

36   For many the continued existence of a Jewish people which does not acknowledge Christ is a divine mystery which finds its only sufficient explanation in the purpose of God's unchanging faithfulness and mercy (Romans ix, 25-29).

3. *Barriers to be overcome*

37   Before our churches can hope to fulfil the commission laid upon us by our Lord there are high barriers to be overcome. We speak here particularly of the barriers which we have too often helped to build and which we alone can remove.

38   We must acknowledge in all humility that too often we have failed to manifest Christian love toward our Jewish neighbours, or even a resolute will for common social justice. We have failed to fight with all our strength the age-old disorder of man which anti-semitism represents. The churches in the past have helped to foster an image of the Jews as the sole enemies of Christ, which has contributed to anti-semitism in the secular world. In many lands virulent anti-semitism still threatens and in other lands the Jews are subjected to many indignities.

39   We call upon all the churches we represent to denounce

anti-semitism, no matter what its origin, as absolutely irreconcilable with the profession and practice of the Christian faith. Anti-semitism is sin against God and man.

Only as we give convincing evidence to our Jewish neighbours that we seek for them the common rights and dignities which God wills for His children, can we come to such a meeting with them as would make it possible to share with them the best which God has given us in Christ.

4.

LUND

Third World Conference
on Faith and Order
August 15-28, 1952

FINAL REPORT

I. A WORD TO THE CHURCHES

1   We have been sent to Lund by our Churches to study together what measure of unity in matters of faith, church order, and worship exists among our Churches and how we may move toward the fuller unity God wills for us. We give thanks to the Lord of the Church for what He has wrought among us in and through our fellowship of conversation and prayer and for evidences that in several parts of the world Churches are drawing closer together. We have made many discoveries about one another's Churches and our perplexity in the face of unresolved differences has been surpassed by our gratitude for the manifold grace of God which we see at work in the life of the Churches all over the world.

2   We have seen clearly that we can make no real advance toward unity if we only compare our several conceptions of the nature of the Church and the traditions in which they are embodied. But once again it has been proved true that as we seek to draw closer to Christ we come closer to one another. We need, therefore, to penetrate behind our divisions to a deeper and richer understanding of the

mystery of the God-given union of Christ with His Church. We need increasingly to realise that the separate histories of our Churches find their full meaning only if seen in the perspective of God's dealings with His *whole* people.

3   We have now reached a crucial point in our ecumenical discussions. As we have come to know one another better our eyes have been opened to the depth and pain of our separations and also to our fundamental unity. The measure of unity which it has been given to the Churches to experience together must now find clearer manifestation. A faith in the one Church of Christ which is not implemented by *acts* of obedience is dead. There are truths about the nature of God and His Church which will remain for ever closed to us unless we act together in obedience to the unity which is already ours. We would, therefore, earnestly request our Churches to consider whether they are doing all they ought to do to manifest the oneness of the people of God. Should not our Churches ask themselves whether they are showing sufficient eagerness to enter into conversation with other Churches and whether they should not act together in all matters except those in which deep differences of conviction compel them to act separately? Should they not acknowledge the fact that they often allow themselves to be separated from each other by secular forces and influences instead of witnessing together to the sole Lordship of Christ who gathers His people out of all nations, races, and tongues?

4   Obedience to God demands also that the Churches seek unity in their mission to the world. We share the failure to convey the Christian message to the mass of mankind. But it is precisely to these masses that we have the obligation to preach the one Gospel, and to manifest the oneness of the Church.

5   The word penitence has been often on our lips here at Lund. Penitence involves willingness to endure judgment— the judgment of the Lord to whom has been given the power to sift mankind and to gather into one the scattered children of God. We await His final triumph at the end of history. But, in God's mercy, tokens of judgment which are also calls to a new and active obedience come to us in our day also, here and now. Surely we cannot any longer remain blind to the signs of our times and deaf to His Word.

6   The Lord says once again: "He that gathereth not with me, scattereth."

II. CHRIST AND HIS CHURCH

7   We believe in Jesus Christ our Lord, who loved the Church and gave himself for it, and has brought the Church into an abiding union with Himself. Because we believe in Jesus Christ, we believe also in the Church as the Body of Christ.

I

8   We confess that without Christ we are lost, and without Him we are subject to the powers of sin and death, but that God has not abandoned us to the powers of destruction. He has given to us and all men His only begotten Son as Saviour and Redeemer. Through His life, His suffering, His death, and His resurrection Jesus Christ as the mighty Victor has overcome sin and death, brought the ungodly powers to nought, and has given us freedom. When we believe in Jesus Christ these powers can no longer exercise lordship over us. Thus we stand under a new Lord. It is Jesus Christ who is our Lord.

9   For He, in His incarnation, death, and resurrection, has entered into oneness with man in his estrangement and in his existence under the judgment of God, and by making atonement for man's guilt has consecrated a new way in which man, reconciled with God, may live in union with Jesus Christ. Through Him God has given to lost humanity a new beginning, for in that Jesus Christ died and rose again, all who believe in Him die and rise again to a new life.

10   Jesus Christ is the King of the new People of God. He is "the chief cornerstone in which the whole building, fitly framed together, grows up into a holy temple in the Lord." He is the head of the Church which is His body. Through His Spirit Jesus Christ Himself is present in His Church. Christ lives in His Church and the Church lives in Christ. Christ is never without His Church; the Church is never without Christ. Both belong inseparably together, the King and His people, the keystone and the temple, the Head and the Body. As members of His Body we are made one with Him in the fellowship of His life, death, and resur-

rection, of His suffering and His glory. For what concerns Christ concerns His Body also. What has happened to Christ uniquely in His once-and-for-all death and resurrection on our behalf, happens also to the Church in its way as His Body. As the Church is made a partaker in the crucified Body of Christ, so also it is given to be partaker in the risen Body of the same Lord. This means that the Church is called to continue the mission of Jesus Christ to the world, so that the way of Christ is the way of His Church.

II

11   On the ground of the apostolic witness to Jesus Christ, the Lord of the Church, and in obedience to Him, we seek to penetrate behind the divisions of the Church on earth to our common faith in the one Lord. From the unity of Christ we seek to understand the unity of the Church on earth, and from the unity of Christ and His Body we seek a means of realising that unity in the actual state of our divisions on earth.

12   We believe that many of our differences arise from a false antithesis between the Church's being in Christ and its mission in the world, and from a failure to understand the Church in the light of Jesus Christ as God and man, and in the light of His death and resurrection. In the following paragraphs we seek:

(1) to speak of the nature of the Church in terms of a double movement (its being called from the world and its being sent into the world) through which it is ever being built up into Jesus Christ its Head; (2) to speak of the Church as the new creation, which while it continues to live on earth as a community of forgiven sinners, expecting the redemption of the body, is already given to participate in the new life of the risen Christ.

The Faith of the Church in the Father,
the Son, and the Holy Spirit

13   In His eternal love the Father has sent His Son to redeem creation from sin and death. In Jesus Christ, God's Son became Man. By word and deed He proclaimed on earth the arrival of God's kingdom, bore away the sins of the world on the Cross, rose again from the dead, ascended into heaven, to the throne of His kingdom, at the

88

right hand of God. At Pentecost God poured out His Spirit upon the Church, giving all who believe in Jesus Christ the power to become God's children. Through the indwelling of His Spirit, Jesus Christ dwells in the midst of His Church. As Lord and King He will come again to judge the quick and the dead and to consummate the eternal kingdom of God in the whole creation.

The Nature and Mission of the Church

14   (a) The Lord Jesus Christ, through His Word and Spirit, calls His Church from the world. He forgives sins, delivers men from the lordship of the powers of destruction and gathers out of this broken world the one People of God, the community of the justified and sanctified whose citizenship is in heaven and whose life is hid with Christ in God.

15   (b) Jesus Christ through His Word and Spirit sends His Church into the world to be the salt of the earth and the light of the world. That is, as Prophet, Priest, and King, He gives His Church to participate in His ministry of reconciliation, constraining it by His love to enter into His passion for the redemption of the world, and empowering it by His Spirit to proclaim the Gospel of Salvation to all nations, calling them to obey the will of God in all the areas of political and social and cultural life and to live out in the divisions of the world the life of the one People of God, so that through its witness Jesus Christ is at work among men as Saviour, and brings all things in subjection under Himself as Lord and King of the world.

16   (c) By calling and sending His People, by granting them manifold spiritual gifts for the ministry, Jesus Christ builds up His Church as the living Temple of God. Thus the Church as the Body of Christ "grows up into him in all things who is the head, from whom the whole Body fitly joined together and compacted by that which every joint supplieth according to the effective working in the measure of every part, maketh increase of the body unto the edifying of itself in love."

The Church between the First and the Final Coming of Christ

17   (a) At the same time the Church is a community of forgiven sinners eagerly expecting and patiently watching for the final consummation of its redemption. It continues to

be a pilgrim people in a strange land, so that all its life and work on earth is incomplete. Ungodly powers and forces are still rampant in the whole creation in an alarming way, and they seek to confuse the Church and defeat its mission. But the Church continues to live and work by the power of Jesus Christ.

18   (b) At the end of its pilgrimage Jesus Christ, the Crucified and Risen, will come again to meet His Church in order to complete His work of redemption and judgment. Out of all peoples and ages He will gather His own who look for His appearing and for a new heaven and a new earth, and He will consummate the union between Christ and His Church in the eternal kingdom of God.

19   (c) Through the indwelling of the Holy Spirit the new age of the future is already present and through union with the risen Jesus Christ the Church on earth is already given to participate in the power of the resurrection. The Church of Jesus Christ in history is at once the congregation of sinners and the new creation, for although it continues to live and work within the brokenness and estrangement of this world and to share in its divisions, the Church belongs essentially to the new age and the new creation. As such the Church is summoned to perpetual renewal, to put off the old life, and by the renewal of its mind to be conformed to Christ, looking beyond its historical forms to the full unveiling of its new being in the coming Lord.

III

20   We have sought to declare in these brief paragraphs the inseparable relation between Christ and His Church. To these convictions about the Church we are led by our faith in Jesus Christ and by our shared acceptance of the authority of the Holy Scriptures. We cannot build the one Church by cleverly fitting together our divided inheritances. We can grow together toward fullness and unity in Christ only by being conformed to Him who is the Head of the Body and Lord of His people. And He manifests His fullness, however brokenly, in the gifts He has given to us even in our separations. Whenever two or three are gathered in His Name, He is in the midst of them. Whenever men are met in obedience to Him, He is known. He may be found in the midst of those from whom we are separated and in the midst of those to whom we are sent.

21   When we place ourselves in our Churches under His judgment and in obedience to His calling and His sending, we shall know that we cannot manifest our unity and share in His fullness without being changed. Some of us who have been assured that we possess the true order and the true sacraments will find ourselves called to give its rightful place to the preaching of the Living Word. Some who have neglected the sacraments will be confronted by Him who humbled Himself in Baptism and broke bread and shared the cup to make us partakers of His passion and death. Those who have sought to show forth the glory of the Church as the Body and Bride of Christ must stand under the judgment of His simplicity and servanthood. Churches which have valued little His prayer that the oneness of His people be made manifest to men will be summoned to make His prayer their own. Churches complacent in the face of racial divisions in the Body will be brought to repentance by Him in whom bond and free, Jew and Gentile, Greek and barbarian, are one. Churches which have stressed one-sidedly that God in His Church gives Himself to men will be reminded that Christ in His humanity offered Himself to the Father. Those who are ever looking backward and have accumulated much precious ecclesiastical baggage will perhaps be shown that pilgrims must travel light and that, if we are to share at last in the great Supper, we must let go much that we treasure. Churches settled and self-assured will have to hear again the Lord's heartbroken concern for the sheep without a shepherd and know that to be His Church is to share in His world-embracing mission. Churches too much at home in the world will hear themselves called out of the world. Churches too wrapped up in their own piety or their own survival will see again Him who identified Himself with the deprived and the oppressed.

22   We cannot know all that shall be disclosed to us when together we look to Him who is the Head of the Body. It is easy for us in our several Churches to think of what our separated brethren need to learn. Christ's love will make us more ready to learn what He can teach us through them. The truth we would hold fast is that because Christ is the Head and Lord of the Church, His way is the Church's way. He calls, He sends, He judges. The shape of His life

is the shape of the Church's life. The mystery of His life is the mystery of the Church's life.

IV

RECOMMENDATION

23   In our work we have been led to the conviction that it is of decisive importance for the advance of ecumenical work that the doctrine of the Church be treated in close relation both to the doctrine of Christ and to the doctrine of the Holy Spirit. We believe that this must occupy a primary place in the future work of this movement, and we so recommend to the Faith and Order Commission, and to its Working Committee.

III. CONTINUITY AND UNITY

I. *The Unity of the Church as indicated in the New Testament*

24   (a) When we think of the unity of the Church in respect of the term "People of God," we are all agreed that we must relate it to the other qualifications of the Church in the New Testament, all of which emphasise the Church's unity.

25   The Church, the newly constituted "People of God," called into being by His Word and His Spirit, is a community in which men recognise the Lordship of the one Christ, which lives by His grace, and which is fully empowered for His service. The Church witnesses to Jesus Christ as the Lord of all life, in its worship, in its order, and in its life. Thus by its nature it is destined, confronting mankind with its divine unity, to triumph over all enmities of nations.

26   This new people of God is described in the New Testament as the Body of Christ. Christ is the Head and He unites all believers in Himself. By the indwelling of the Holy Spirit the redeemed are united into a body, in the world but not of it, as a "People of God's own possession," who share in common the gifts of the one Spirit. Since the Church is a fellowship in the Holy Spirit, it follows that it is a *communio sanctorum*, a company of the sanctified—forgiven, justified by faith, and born anew in Christ.

27   (b) (i) All the various testimonies of faith in Christ

92

found in the New Testament express one and the same faith, and all of them together belong to the revelation of God in Him.

28   (ii) While there are indications of diversity in worship in the New Testament, nevertheless the preaching of the Word and the administration of Baptism and the Lord's Supper were everywhere marks of the Church's unity.

29   (iii) We all believe that God gives to His Church unity in a rich diversity of works of mercy, moral and social witness, and prophetic insight into human affairs. He united His Church in a love for the brethren and for all mankind which transcends every barrier of race, colour, class, and nation.

30   (iv) In the New Testament the mission of the Church and the unity of the Church are deeply related. Christ called His apostles that they might be one and that He might send them forth to accomplish His mission in the world. He prayed for their unity that the world might believe. It was in obedience to this missionary task, including the willingness to suffer for Christ, that the Church experienced the dynamic power of its unity.

31   (v) The subject of church order, both in its New Testament phases and in its subsequent history, is treated in the following section.

II. *Unity, Continuity, and Discontinuity*
(1) The Unity of Christ and His Church

32   Life in the Church rests upon the operation of the Triune God but (as we have seen in Chapter II) there is a special need to examine the relationship of the Church to Christ. To quote from the Report of the Theological Commission on the Church:

"Every communion holds that the Church is not a human contrivance, but God's gift for the salvation of the world, that the saving acts of God in Christ brought it into being, that it persists in continuity in history by the presence and power of the Holy Spirit."

33   The discussion of unity and continuity involves, therefore, the prior question of the nature of the relationship between Christ and the Church. The continuity of the Church is based upon the fact that Christ is her Head and that, therefore, there is but one holy Catholic and Apostolic Church, which has not only received the promise of Christ that

93

"the gates of hell shall not prevail against it," but also receives, as partaker of His resurrection, the earnest of her future triumph.

34   The Pauline image of the Church as the Body of Christ is no mere metaphor, but expresses a living reality. All agree in finding the presence of Jesus Christ, the crucified and risen Lord, both living in and reigning over His Church. She is created as the realm of redemption by the sovereign grace of God and is also the sphere of His acts of judgment and reformation. We unite in affirming the solidarity between the Head and the members and also the sovereignty of the Head over the members in the Body of Christ. But there are differing emphases among us as to the differing modes of participation of the members in the Head. The former view stresses the fullness of Christ as something already received by the Church, though not always consciously apprehended, the latter the manifestation of his same fullness at the Coming of the Lord in glory. In the present age, however, it is in the Church under the Cross that the fullness of Christ is realised.

(2) The Nature of Continuity

35   From this difference of emphasis arise different opinions upon the nature of continuity. All agree not only upon the continuity assured by the constant action of the risen Lord through the Holy Spirit, but also upon the value of some form of continuity in history, assured by some means under the action of the Holy Spirit. All would emphasise the apostolic continuity of Christian life within the Christian community of men and women, redeemed by the one Cross of Christ, seeking to follow the example and teaching of the same Master and inspired by the continuing presence of the same living Lord. Most would also regard the preaching of the Gospel and the ministration of the sacraments as essential means of continuity.

36   While the vast majority of Christians would agree that some form of commissioned ministry was essential to the continuing life of the Church, serious and at present irreconcilable disagreement arises on the question whether some particular form of ministerial order is essential to the continuity of the Church.

37   It is clear then that nearly all communions possess and cherish some form of ministry for which in some way they

find warrant in the New Testament.[1] Many would go further and find in the various forms of ministry which they already exercise a continuation of the mission of the Apostles. A special significance is, however, attached by some Churches to the possession of the historic episcopate in apostolic succession. Some, indeed, possess and value this without attaching any necessary doctrinal significance to it. For others, however, all other means of continuity are here focussed and they would regard common acceptance of a ministry in this succession as an essential step towards the unity of the Church and as the only sufficient safeguard of its historic continuity. The kind or degree of doctrinal interpretation implied in such an acceptance is still a matter of disagreement. Others would find apostolic succession to be one element in an organic structure of life and worship, faith and order, which, in their totality, constitute the principle of continuity.

38   It is clear that here is an obstinate difference, held with deep conviction and in a good conscience, which cannot readily be resolved. It is possible, however, to note some growth together. Churches which have not in the past been much given to the consideration of this question are finding greater value in an emphasis upon the idea and content of continuity than in former times, while Churches which emphasise particular forms of continuity as essential are finding the need to integrate more closely in their thinking the two elements of Faith and Order. We recall the words of the Report of the Lausanne Conference, which called for "a ministry acknowledged by every part of the Church of Christ as possessing not only the inward call of the Spirit, but also the commission of Christ and the authority of the whole Body." Some would hold that we have passed beyond this point in seeking a more precise content to the term "ministry." Here clearly a fresh starting-point to theological

[1] The evidence of the New Testament about church order can be variously interpreted.
(a) Some believe that already in the New Testament we find a development from the apostolic order towards episcopacy, despite the existence of other forms of ministering, subject to the apostolic tradition.
(b) Others hold that while there is evidence of variety of order in the New Testament, the general trend is not towards episcopacy but towards other forms of order (e.g., congregational or presbyteral), and they would claim that Churches of these types of order reflect more nearly the primitive tradition.
(c) In the opinion of others again no clear line of development of ecclesiastical order can be discerned in the New Testament. Leadership within the Christian community accords with the varying needs of the Church but is always closely correlated with the responsibility of members and subject to the authority of Christ as Lord.
Recent biblical study has, however, led to a considerable growth together on the whole question.

discussion is urgently needed. An approach to the question of the ministry, not as an isolated phenomenon but in the light of a profound Christological and eschatological approach to the doctrine of the Church, is urgently needed. Beyond our theological and denominational emphases, we must seek to keep our eyes fixed upon Christ as Prophet, Priest, and King and find in the vision of Him the focal point of ways which at present appear merely parallel.

39   We propose the establishment of a Theological Commission to explore more deeply the resources for further ecumenical discussion to be found in that common history which we have as Christians and which we have discovered to be longer, larger, and richer than any of our separate histories in our divided Churches. Such a study would focus not only on the hard cores of disagreement between us, but also on the positive discoveries there to be made of the various levels of unity which underlie our diversities and dividedness.

(3) Discontinuity

40   A consideration of the nature of continuity can only serve to throw into stronger relief the fact of discontinuity and the factors which have led historically to it.

41   (a) *Schism.* The term "schism" appears to be used in two different senses. Some maintain that it can only be used of a breach between Church organisations of an identical or closely similar pattern of life, faith and order, whether arising from political, cultural, or even personal reasons, and leading to administrative or jurisdictional separation, total or partial. In this view, the term "schism" would not be used in cases where matters of heresy were involved. Others, however, are accustomed to use the term in a wider sense to cover the separation of Christian groups on matters of doctrine (e.g. the Reformation). There appears to be a real need for the introduction of another agreed term for such division. Terms like "breach" (in English), "rupture" (in French), "*Spaltung*" (in German), are possible, but for various reasons they cannot be regarded as fully satisfactory. In further study of this question the need is felt to discover words which as far as possible reflect the living nature of the Church.

42   The use of the terms "heretic" and "schismatic" between Christians is happily passing out of current usage, but the

growth of mutual respect and charity and the desire for fuller unity with each other should not obscure the need for a serious consideration of the nature of division. We are all agreed that "tragic" is not too strong a word to express the effect of these divisions; that they sometimes become necessary is a sign of the presence of sin in the world. All would agree that a conflict of "goods" as well as a choice of evils may be involved in some separations. To quote but one example: the Reformation is interpreted by many primarily as an act of obedience to God, while others will find involved in it a sinful breaking of the unity of the Church.

43   While many Churches would willingly recognise in the origin of their divisions, all would find in their maintenance, a matter in which our guilt is not one-sided but reciprocal. Some divisions arose from vital matters of Christian truth and life, others from impatience on the one side, and lack of understanding and vitality on the other—the refusal of a church to reform itself or to meet new spiritual demands made upon it by its people and its historical situation. Sometimes divisions have occurred by the joint action of ecclesiastical and secular powers, issuing in persecution. There are also divisions which do not fall easily into these classifications, and which are due in the main to social, cultural, or racial tensions. We wish to call attention to the obligation to seek closer organic union which specially lies upon (a) Churches whose close regional association emphasises their task of bearing a common witness to the non-Christian world; (b) Churches whose historic past lays upon them to a peculiar degree the need for mutual reconciliation; (c) Churches having a close doctrinal or institutional affinity. While, however, we stress the importance of a reunion of Churches of closer spiritual heritage, we do not forget the need for, and the possibility of, a reunion of wider scope, which may bring together those of very different spiritual heritage. We particularly deplore the tendency to create further divisions in some parts of the world, often for the flimsiest of reasons, which, while we seek a closer unity, threatens to produce an even more disastrous situation.

44   Of recent years it has been widely maintained that our breaches as Christian denominations are rather breaches within than from the Church. Such a view can hardly be

received by those who, for varying reasons, maintain that the *una sancta* (the one holy Catholic and Apostolic Church) cannot be broken, or by those who restrict the limits of the visible Church of Christ to a single denomination. Others, however, are prepared to see in this distinction a welcome affirmation of the continued existence of church life on both sides of the breach. It was maintained, for example, that on each side of the breach there existed a *traditio ministrandi* (an ordered pattern of ministry of the Christian faith) and a profession of the Christian faith itself, although in either case it might be possible to find elements which really belong together held in isolation or even set in sharp opposition to each other. In a divided Christendom, there is an inescapable tension between our commission to exercise our ministry in the whole Church of Christ and its present restriction to the confines of a single denomination. A doctrinal protest can easily become a fixed theology. Such breaches, if always involving loss, do not necessarily mean total shipwreck and it is the duty of all to look forward to a new integration of life and faith and a fulfilment of ministries in future steps towards organic unity. For some the problem of the divided Church and its reunion is linked to the question of *vestigia ecclesiae* (the characteristics of the universal Church still existing in the divided Churches). Here is an urgent problem for ecumenical research.

45 (b) *Apostasy.* Apostasy may be defined as in essence a denial of the sole Lordship of Christ in profession, attitude, or action. Any loyalty, however innocent in itself, when exalted to the point where it conflicts with loyalty to God in Christ, tends towards apostasy. It is thus a manifestation of satanic power rebelling against God. It may take the positive form of aggressive rebellion against God or the more negative form of a lukewarm allegiance to Him. A special danger lies in the fact that apostasy sometimes clothes itself in a Christian vocabulary and outwardly Christian forms. The determination and judgment of apostasy belong to God and only pertain to the Church as revealed by Him. Today a peculiar urgency attaches to the duty of the Church to reaffirm her sole loyalty to Christ in the face of the insidious advance of secularism, the challenge of a state absolutism which seeks to control the thought forms of the human individual and challenges the possibility of his whole existence as a Christian, and the menace of oppression in all its forms (political, economic, or even ecclesiastical) in all parts of the world. Apostasy is a danger against which our denominations as a whole and ourselves as individuals ought to be watchful rather than a defect that we should wish to point out in others.

46   In the minds of some the possibility of widespread or even of total apostasy is closely linked to the problem of discontinuity. Some Churches might possess the strongest possible outward form of continuity and yet in whole or in part be affected by apostasy. It is more normally held, however, that apostasy can take place either in an individual or in a Christian group, but it is not generally believed that the whole Church could ever fall into apostasy.

47   (c) *Heresy.* In the history of the Church heresy and division have often been closely connected. Christian teaching is always integrally related to Christian life, worship, and action, just as in New Testament times the *kerygma* (proclamation), *koinonia* (fellowship) and the *diakonia* (Christian service) are not found in separation from each other. Properly speaking, heresy belongs to the first sphere alone and may be defined as an error of doctrine persistently proclaimed against an established norm of the Church, affecting vital matters of teaching. Since, however, life and thought, worship and action, are inseparable, it involves a distortion of the spiritual life of the Church and of the organic wholeness of the Christian faith. It is agreed that there are *necessaria* (necessary articles) in the Christian faith and we would restrict the word "heresy" to this sphere, but we are not unanimous about their number and nature. We all recognise the obligation upon the Churches, while seeking to maintain in all its fullness the deposit of faith, to be responsive to the guidance of the Holy Spirit as He fulfils our Lord's promise to lead His Church into all truth and to bear continual witness to Him.

48   In all matters judgment should properly belong to the whole visible Church of Christ, but in our divided state this judgment can and must be exercised by individual denominations and even congregations, acting through all their parts or, as others would say, orders. Every effort must be made pastorally and spiritually for the reconciliation of the offender. If, however, sentence must in the last resort be passed upon him, we are united in repudiating

any recourse to secular coercion and violence. The nature of the doctrinal norms by which heresy is to be judged are treated later in this chapter.

III. *Unity and Diversity*

49   (a) *Personal faith in Jesus Christ.* Faith in Jesus Christ as Lord and Saviour, the original simple New Testament affirmation, is confessed by all the communions here represented. This common faith allows for certain differences of interpretation and practice.

50   (b) *Consensus in doctrine.* All accept the Holy Scriptures as either the sole authority for doctrine or the primary and decisive part of those authorities to which they would appeal. Most accept the Ecumenical Creeds as an interpretation of the truth of the Bible or as marking a distinctive stage in the working-out of the orthodox faith. Some assign a special importance to the creedal documents of the early Ecumenical Councils. Some would say that to found unity on any creeds is to found it on something human, namely, our understanding of the Gospel and our theological work in formulating its meaning. Some judge in accordance with the Inner Light and the leadings of the Spirit and are therefore concerned to witness against the use of outward creeds when these are held to be necessary or sufficient.

51   Many denominations possess confessional documents in which they express the Christian Faith as they read it in the Bible. It would generally be admitted, however, that these last documents would not be regarded as irreformable and they do not in fact occupy the same position in the Rule of Faith of all Churches which possess them.

52   We acknowledge the importance of theological study for intellectual clarification and continuous re-interpretation of the Christian faith in terms of changing life and thought. In listening to one another in ecumenical discussion we move towards a deeper understanding of each other in faith and doctrine.

53   (c) *Forms of worship and the sacraments.* The subject of forms of worship and the sacraments is treated in the next chapter.[2]

[2]It should be noted throughout this report that most Baptists would prefer to use the term "ordinance" rather than "sacrament."

54   (d) *Evangelism.* The Church by its very nature is an evangelizing fellowship with an inescapable missionary obligation.

There is among us a difference of opinion as to whether a Church has the right to evangelize members of another Christian communion. While some of us deny that such a right exists, others claim that it is an essential part of their mission. There are forms of proselytising, however, which are sub-Christian and should, therefore, find no place among the followers of our One Lord. In the United Church this problem would find its solution.

55   (e) *The Christian life.* We acknowledge that the Christian experience of God's redemptive grace finds its expression in Christian life in a variety of ways. We are agreed as to the necessity of witnessing for Christ, by word and deed in every human relationship. Service prompted and guided by love is the primary characteristic of the Christian way of living, and life's true interpretation is to be found in the idea that we are stewards of our Lord. We rejoice in the new emphasis upon the fact that our daily work is a sacred vocation or an offering to God.

56   (f) *Cultural factors.* We recognise that Christianity makes itself at home in various cultures and takes a colouring from them. We believe that every nation will bring its tribute to the common treasury of Christian faith and life. Christianity is never to be equated with any culture, however, for it has a spirit of its own which always transcends social, political, and cultural conditions. The Spirit creates unity, while one of the causes of division lies in treating as absolute cultural factors which are only relative.

57   We call upon the Churches honestly to face certain present social and cultural conditions which greatly accentuate the need for unity, e.g., the general disorder of human society, new migrations of population, the redrawing of political boundaries, state antagonism and persecution, the assumption by the modern state of responsibility for education and social work, and the achievement of national independence by countries in which the Churches were founded by Western missionary expansion.

58   While we recognise that social and cultural factors have operated most significantly to produce divisions among us, we call attention also to the fact that they have sometimes been the occasion of overcoming previously

101

existing divisions. The unity found by Christians as a result of persecution is a striking illustration of this truth.

59   (g) *Varying degrees of recognition.* There is considerable variation in the degree of recognition accorded by one Christian body to another. Within the same confessional family it is customary to regard other regional and national Churches as Christian Churches in the full sense of the word. But full recognition in many instances is not extended outside the same confessional family. For example:

(1) Some Churches do not usually extend to others outside their tradition the right of participation in their sacramental life.

(2) When a member of one Church in good standing desires to transfer to another communion, some Churches require rebaptism or a new profession of faith.

(3) When a minister desires to transfer from one communion to another, some Churches require re-ordination.

60   Membership in the World Council of Churches implies a measure of recognition in that the Churches recognise one another as serving one Lord. But differences of faith and order still exist and membership in the Council does not imply that one Church must regard all other members as Churches in the full sense.

61   A more general form of recognition is extended, on the other hand, by the very fact of joining, in mutual respect, for the study of differences, engaging in co-operative endeavour in Christian action and missions, and occasionally gathering in common worship. In these and other ways Christians recognise one another as belonging to the Body of Christ and pray that they may grow by God's grace into greater unity and more complete mutual recognition.

IV. *The Unity We Have and the Unity We Seek*

62   We affirm that throughout Christendom there is, despite divisions, a unity already given by God in Christ; through whom "the powers of the age to come" are already in our midst. Concerning the fact of this unity and of the participation in it of every Christian we have no doubt. The co-operation in the Ecumenical Movement is one practical proof that this unity is here. We affirm also our faith that the crucified and risen Christ is already working through His Holy Spirit to deliver us from the divisions which obscure this unity, and our sure hope that at His return in

glory He will enable the manifestation of this unity to be complete. This very hope lays upon us all the inescapable duty of working and praying for the shortening of the days of our separation, in obedience to Him in whom we affirm ourselves to be one.

63   We differ, however, in our understanding of the relation of our unity in Christ to the visible holy Catholic and Apostolic Church. We are agreed that there are not two Churches, one visible and the other invisible, but one Church which must find visible expression on earth, but we differ in our belief as to whether certain doctrinal, sacramental, and ministerial forms are of the essence of the Church itself. In consequence, we differ in our understanding of the character of the unity of the Church on earth for which we hope though none of us looks forward to an institution with a rigid uniformity of governmental structure and all of us look forward to a time when all Christians can have unrestricted communion in Sacrament and fellowship with each other.

64   Yet our difference in the doctrinal and sacramental content of our faith and of our hope do not prevent us from being one in the act of believing and of hoping. For our faith and our hope are in the crucified and risen Jesus Christ, who is already working in us the purpose of His perfect will, and is already gathering up every fragment of obedient endeavour into the consummation of that purpose.

V. *Illustrations of United Advance*

65   We believe that it is God's will that we should be united, and we see in the urgent problems and the desperate needs of the whole modern world new calls and opportunities to hear the unifying Word of God.

66   In making recommendations that we hope will be effective without raising disagreements of principle, we yet recognise that all our working together is in greater or less measure impeded by the divisions among us created by our disagreements on faith and order. Within the Ecumenical Movement which has exposed our disagreements, we have none the less become aware of a definite area of unity, and it is being laid upon us by the Holy Spirit and the Word of God to come together increasingly in His service.

103

67   We make these recommendations in the conviction that we should do together all that can be done together, and do separately only that which must be done separately. Some of the recommendations that follow are elaborated in the Report of the Second Conference on Faith and Order held in Edinburgh in 1937.[3]

68   1. We believe that the deliverance of this world from its religious disunion and bitter secular feuds can be achieved by Christians capable of presenting the practical challenges of Christian love to the self-interest in Churches and groups, and able to persist without the visible and immediate expectation of success. It is the task of Christian communions to make known the call of God to their members to this ministry of reconciliation and to sustain them by bringing to them in their courage and loneliness the fellowship of the faith.

69   2. The separated communions will be helped to come together into the cause of Christian service by realising that the emotional legacy, which hinders their co-operating, is to a considerable extent the result of what have been called "non-theological factors of denominationalism." These are traditions of a political, national, and social character. Awareness of these factors is the first step in ridding ourselves of the divisive feelings that they have aroused. We therefore urge on religious communions wishing to co-operate a special study of these hindrances.

70   One factor calling for special study is the tradition of establishment, which in some countries continues to be a source of division among the Churches.

71   3. We recognise that many of the most pressing and troubling problems of the modern world have arisen subsequent to the forming of our separate traditions of faith and order. They cannot therefore be dealt with adequately from within our traditional divisions. The Churches of to-day have to help each other answer their problems. Individuals equipped with special knowledge and spiritual insight to relate Christian teaching to these problems belong to the whole Church, and such messengers should be given greater opportunities to be heard by all Christian people.

72   4. We believe that the needs of our modern world call for closer fellowship and co-operation between those who serve God and their fellow men in the offices and specific

[3] cf. Ed 160-187.

activities of the Church and those who, consciously or not, (73-75) serve God and their fellow men in other ways.

76   8. In view of the complexity of modern problems for Christian decision, we recommend united study groups for Christians living in the same locality and at work in the same occupational groups. We recommend also the formation and support of local 'Councils of Churches' for consultation and joint action. The Ecumenical Movement is (77-81) not alive unless it is local. . . .

82   14. We ask for a greater observance on the part of all Christians of the designated periods of corporate prayer for Christian unity and ask the responsible authorities to arrange if possible for a co-ordination of weeks of prayer for unity.

83   We believe that we should thank God for His gift in bringing into existence the World Council of Churches. We must not overestimate its significance, but still less should we overlook the fact that in it God has given us, for manifesting our fellowship and common responsibility, an instrument which is unique in history.

84   God has brought us together in years of war and occupation, in prisons and camps, in areas of orphan missions, and for works of relief and reconstruction. In many quarters we have been brought nearer to each other by a rediscovery of the full message of the Gospel, of the Church, its worship and sacraments, and its service to the world. New forms of Christian community life have sprung up within various denominations. They are the promising signs of the ongoing renewing and uniting work of the Spirit throughout Christ's Church Universal.

85   In all of these advances the World Council of Churches has acted as a pervasive influence. Through it God, we believe, continues to call us, in the realms of fellowship and united service, to speak the word that is not yet spoken and do the deed that is not yet done.

VI. *Summary and Prospect*

86   In summary, the nature of the unity towards which we are striving is that of a visible fellowship in which all members, acknowledging Jesus Christ as living Lord and Saviour, shall recognise each other as belonging fully to His Body, to the end that the world may believe.

87   In His own day Jesus Christ will gather His scattered

people to live in eternal union with Him. The joy of that union is already felt in such unitedness as is now ours. With light that pierces the Christian conscience that day of our Lord illuminates the solemn responsibility of every contemporary communion to prepare itself for unity.

Further study

88   Some of us hold that the unity of the Church must be organic as being the unity of the Body of Christ. That Body must be composed of elements belonging to this world of space and time but these elements must be unified as the Body of the Lord by the unifying power of His indwelling Spirit; otherwise it would not be organic. At first sight this conception seems utterly opposed to the notion of a union of distinct Churches. But a covenant relationship *realised to the full* would bind the Churches together into the organic unity of the Body of Christ, because it would be a relationship *in Christo,* the indwelling *Creator Spiritus* unifying the distinct members.

89   There are others, however, who hold that to speak of a "covenant" between denominations of Christians is to use the word "covenant" in a way which is far removed from the Biblical usage and conception. They would emphasise the finality of the "covenant" once made by God through Christ, and would urge that the task of Christian unity is to make effective our common response to that covenant. We believe that this is a most fruitful field for further study.

IV. WAYS OF WORSHIP

Preamble

90   The decision of the Edinburgh Conference to appoint a Theological Commission on Ways of Worship has proved to be an important step forward in the process of mutual understanding necessary to progress in Christian unity. The work of the Commission has strengthened the conviction that Worship, no less than Faith and Order, is essential to the being of the Church. It has also made it clear that disunity is as manifest in the differing ways of worship as in disagreements concerning doctrines and institutions. In-

deed it is at this point that disunity becomes explicit and the sense of separation most acute.

91   Following on the work of the Commission, we attempt here to assess the measure of existing agreement and disagreement as to the meaning and practice of Worship; to consider the bearing of this on the Unity of the Church; and to suggest practical measures for the increase of mutual understanding.

Agreements

92   (1) We worship one God, Father, Son and Holy Spirit, the Triune God, by whose Spirit all true worship is inspired and unto whom all Christian worship is offered.

93   (2) God Himself creates the faith by which we respond to Him in worship, by encountering us and speaking to us. (*Cf.* Gal. 2:20.) By this we mean that at the moment of Christ's encounter with men, they are free to respond; but in the light of this response they understand that they could not have been seeking God had He not already found them, and that the faith by which they responded was itself God's gift to them.

94   (3) God's encounter with us, and the response to Him in worship, involves the whole man. (*Cf.* Matt. 22:37-40.) It is made in worship, in witness and in Christian obedience and service.

95   (4) The response as expressed in Worship involves adoration, confession, hearing the Word of God, intercession, invocation, oblation, praise, supplication, and thanksgiving.

96   (5) Word and Sacrament are both the gifts of God. In the reading and the preaching of the Word and the administration of the sacraments, God offers us His grace, imparts saving knowledge of Himself, and draws us into communion with Himself.

The members of the Society of Friends testify to the same experience through corporate silent worship and lay ministry arising therein.

97   (6) All worship is by and within the family of God's people, alike in heaven and on earth. Even in private prayer, the Christian is always praying with the Church as a member of the communion of saints. The worship of the congregation is both the basis of all private prayer and

devotion, and a powerful and essential Christian witness to the world.

Unsolved Problems

100 (1) Differences of opinion as to the relation of Word and Sacrament have led to varying stresses upon the importance of preaching and the sacraments. This should never be more than a matter of emphasis. God's redeeming activity takes place in the worship which He has established in His Church. The unity of worship ought to be stressed if we are to have it in its fullness.

101 (2) We all agree that worship concerns the whole of life. Yet, we give different emphases to the place in worship of things we can touch and see. For some, many earthly elements when blessed may have a quasi-sacramental use; for others, only the elements which the Lord has appointed ought to play a distinctive role in worship. Therefore the use of material things must be carefully studied in the light of our agreement that Christian worship takes place as the Triune God makes Himself known to His people in Word and Sacrament. Through the Holy Spirit God comes to His people redeeming not only them, but also in some sense, the whole creation.

102 (3) The precise classification of all forms of worship as *"liturgical"* and *"non-liturgical"* is difficult. Indeed the term "liturgical" must be understood as having a wider meaning than is implied in this distinction. Most forms of worship are in a sense liturgical. The real difficulty is between Churches having a set liturgy and those allowing more freedom to the individual minister.

103 Our conversations have revealed that there is a place and value for both. On the one hand the fixed form helps to maintain and hand on the heritage of belief and devotion. On the other hand there are times when much greater freedom is both desired and desirable. Furthermore it is the task of the Church to use liturgical prayer as a means of disciplining the private prayer of the individual, and enlarging the scope of his intercession; while the private prayer of the individual, in its turn, quickens the liturgical life and purges it from the taint of formalism.

104 In both, of course, it is all, in the end, the work of the Holy Spirit.

105   (4) Worship is always the worship of the whole people of God, the whole Church. The leadership of this worship can on some occasions be entrusted to any member. Yet most of our Churches believe that our Lord has called forth in His Church a stated ministry. To this ministry alone the leadership of certain acts of worship is restricted. This raises for us the question of the basis of this restriction. For some of us this restriction rests upon the belief that the Church by the guidance of the Holy Spirit calls some of its members to this or that function. For others it is based upon the belief that the Holy Spirit gives to some members of the Church the appropriate grace of holy order. Again, some Churches emphasise the ministerial priesthood as definitely distinct from the priesthood of all believers.

106   We recognise that questions regarding the character of the ministry, priestly and prophetic, continue to be grave obstacles to unity. Behind them lie fundamental problems concerning the nature of grace and the person and work of Christ. These questions must be faced fully and frankly. Fruitful discussion here may well render less intractable the differences in defining the meaning of apostolic ministry and validity.

107   (5) Whatever may be our various opinions on the nature and efficacy of ritual acts, we are all agreed that *Deus non alligatur sacramentis,* and that (in the words of the Gospel) "the wind bloweth where it listeth . . . so is everyone that is born of the Spirit" (St. John 3:8). We record in thankfulness that we have reached in our discussions a measure of understanding, which none of us could ever have anticipated, on the problem of the sacrificial element in Holy Communion. The mystery of the love of God, which we celebrate at the Lord's Table, surpasses human expression. But in our attempts to describe that mystery we have the warrant of Holy Scripture for using sacrificial language. "Behold the Lamb of God. . . ."

108   Our Lord Jesus Christ in all His life on earth and chiefly in His death and resurrection has overcome the powers of darkness. In His one perfect and sufficient sacrifice on Calvary He offered perfect obedience to the Father in atonement for the sin of the whole world. This was an act of expiation made once and for all and is un-

109

repeatable. In His risen and ascended life He ever makes intercession for us.

109   Our response in worship, then, is the praise, prayer, thanksgiving, and offering of ourselves in faith and obedience made to the Father in the name of Jesus Christ. We make the sacrifice of praise and thanksgiving. It is at this point that our greatest difficulties arise as we seek to express just how our worship on earth is related to the eternal intercession of Christ in heaven. We all agree that there is an element of mystery here which can scarcely be expressed (Rom. 8:26).

110   Some of us believe that in the Lord's Supper, where they enter into communion with the crucified and risen Lord, they only offer a sacrifice of praise and thanksgiving and obedient service as a response in faith to the benefits the Lord gives us. Others would like to insist, however, that in the Holy Eucharist the Lord Jesus Christ as our Great High Priest unites the oblation made by His body, the Church, with His own sacrifice, and so takes up her own adoration into the *Sanctus* of the company of heaven. Between these two views there are others to which a brief reference may not do full justice.

111   It is felt, however, that a deeper understanding of the meaning of "unities" in the above paragraph, particularly in the light of Biblical eschatology, might help to resolve real divergence and misunderstanding at this point.

112   N.B.—There are those among us who regret that the discussion of the Eucharist has concentrated on this sacrificial aspect. In their opinion the main issue is the real bodily presence of the crucified and risen Lord and our receiving of His body and blood.

113   (6) We are agreed in believing in the Communion of Saints as the fellowship of the whole company of believers on earth and in heaven. In its worship, the Church on earth joins in prayer and praise with angels and archangels and all the company of heaven. While all agree in accepting the communion of saints in this sense, there is grave difference of interpretation. Some use the word "saints" only to mean the whole Christian body in general. Others also use it in a special sense to denote the blessed saints in heaven.

114   Most people are ready to sing hymns of thanksgiving for the saints, thanking God for His victory in the lives of His people. Some would go further and venerate the saints in

110

heaven to the extent of celebrating their feasts; still others would seek their intercession believing that they can help us who are still engaged in the earthly warfare. For many of those who venerate the saints, the Blessed Virgin Mary has a unique place. It is obvious that the status of the Blessed Virgin in Christian worship is a matter on which there is deep divergence.

115　We must recognise that for some this aspect of worship is an expression of love flowing through Christ's mystical body. Others believe that such usages would be contrary to their understanding of the whole of Christian faith, and they neither know nor desire any intercessor other than their Saviour.

116　It is therefore clear that these issues can be discussed properly only in the context of the doctrine of grace and of the work of Christ and of the Holy Spirit.

117　Another divergence of view emerges in connection with the practice of prayers for the departed. Some hold that the departed require the help of our prayers, and that we are in charity bound to pray for them that the work of God begun in them may be brought to perfection. Others hold that in committing their beloved dead to the care of the God who gave His only Son to be the Saviour of sinners they may find joy and comfort in His love.

118　This matter also is one which demands most thorough theological work touching as it does the heart of redeeming grace.

Non-Theological Factors

119　Thus far this chapter has been concerned largely with the theology which underlies the agreements and disagreements in ways of worship. In considering our differences, however, we have been constrained to ask whether they spring, wholly or in part, from social, cultural, and other factors. In what follows we offer suggestions toward a new line of approach which may help the Churches to see that many of the differences in ways of worship are not bound up, as has been thought, with irreconcilable dogmatic differences, but may co-exist in one Church.

120　The Churches on earth are *in via,* and therefore involved at every level in the tensions and conflicts of history. This involvement shows itself in their traditions of worship. Even the most cursory survey of these "ways of worship"

111

reveals the large part played by many sorts of non-theological factors.

121   In this statement we intend to concentrate on two of these, the *social* and *psychological*. At certain very important points these overlap as cause-factors making for the estrangement of Christian bodies. For instance, there is the crucial factor of language which operates both psychologically and socially. Round the expressions in a language there tends to gather a whole fabric of associations which are lost in translation, but which colour the use of the expressions in prayer and worship. Moreover, habits of worship differ from country to country. We have all heard of worshipers who complain that they cannot abide the "foreign ways" of the people of such and such a land at prayer. The style of behaviour seems to get in the way of the stranger's devotion. Here too we have an overlap of psychological and social factors.

122   It would be a great mistake to suppose that such intimacy of relation between faith and cultural tradition is a bad thing. On the contrary it often makes for health and vivacity of spiritual tradition. But because human beings are sinners, we have to reckon with the possibility of profound corruption here. A particular Church may unconsciously, in liturgical forms, take for granted social and political institutions which have received drastic criticism at once in theory and practice. For instance, certain clauses of the Anglican Litany belong to a quite different ordering of society from that of Great Britain today. A stranger must be puzzled, even antagonised by such archaism. In a divided Christendom such phenomena can easily create the impression that reconciliation between Churches involves the acceptance of what belongs to the accidents of their worldly history rather than to the vital substance of their faith. This is particularly serious when members of Christian Churches "have done one another wrong" in conflicts which were social and political as well as religious in origin. What is needed here is a certain theological ruthlessness, combined with the realisation that, in the providence of God, what now seems to divide at this level can be so transformed as to enrich the experience of the whole people of God. For it is in His will that His Church has been placed in the world and in the midst of secular history. "I pray not that thou shouldst take them

112

out of the world: but that thou shouldst keep them from the evil one."

123   It must be emphasised, however, that these political and social factors operate not merely to postpone re-union, but frequently contribute to hinder evangelism and to damage the internal life of individual Churches. Thus within the same Church there are often great differences of idiom between congregations recruited from different social classes. While there are perhaps signs of improvement discernible, one cannot neglect the many unhappy examples within Churches of discrimination practised on grounds of class, economic level, politics, and race. When these are continued to the present or actually introduced *de novo*, existing divisions are not only hardened, but Churches are split on occasion into additional fragments.

124   Archaism of devotional habit also prevents the development of the sort of liturgical forms suitable to the age in which we live. For instance, we do well to question what the view of nature implicit in the canticle *Benedicite* conveys to men equipped with skill to effect the colossal transformations of natural forces which are a commonplace of our day. It is not only the cause of Christian unity that compels us to rigorous and painful self-scrutiny at these points: it is the cause of evangelism itself that demands we sit in judgment on our forms of worship. Christian worship must indeed not be subordinated to the fluctuating requirements of human nature; it has its background in God's initiative and His revelation. But its gracious content must be presented in a manner congruent with the actualities of our common life.

125   The study of social factors in their impact upon our ways of worship is in its infancy. Its prosecution is a commanding duty of the Ecumenical Movement. When we pass to the *psychological* side of our statement we come to a field in which we are at present perhaps even more amateurs. At least, however, we must note the importance as a force of division of the attraction felt by some and the repulsion felt by others, when an elaborate ritual is used which seems designed to evoke a sense of mystery. There are many both learned and simple who find their imaginations stimulated by such symbolism; others mistrust what seems to them to savour of trickery and an assault on their emotions. Here the puritan and not seldom the man of science are at one

113

in their reactions; both show a singleminded repudiation of what seems to them obscure, unreal, and artificial. Their challenge is an important one and it cannot be dismissed as simply philistine. There is need for a thorough exploration of the concept of mystery in its bearing on worship, an exploration at once theological, metaphysical, and psychological. This exploration would, of course, have to consider not only the way in which craving for mystery is met in elaborate liturgical worship, but also the way in which it is met in the charismatic forms characteristic of Pentecostalists and others, whose life can easily be ignored by the theologically sophisticated. It remains sadly true that among Christians the willingness to submit their devotional preferences to any kind of psychological scrutiny is rare; until it is more common, we are not perhaps likely to advance far in liberating ourselves from the dominion of what can be merely a matter of personal choice or chance inheritance. Until we have attempted this, it is open to question how far we stand under the sovereignty of faith and are ready to meet the demands made upon us in this age.

RECOMMENDATIONS

126   The Churches may be asked to follow up the work of the Commission on Ways of Worship on the following lines:

(a) The cultivation of a sympathetic and reverent attitude by all Christian people toward all forms of worship, both "liturgical" and "non-liturgical," in which God confronts man.

(b) Detailed scrutiny of the grounds upon which the worship of each communion is based, and in this light the re-examination of its attitude to that of others.

(c) Reflection on the question: How far does the fact that there are varieties in forms of worship within the same communions make it possible to conceive of a similar rich diversity within a united Church?

(d) Study of the liturgical movements going on in various parts of the world, coupled with study of the roots of modern antagonism to Christian worship in all its forms.

(e) Thorough examination of the relationship between the unique sacrifice of Jesus Christ and man's response in worship and life.

(f) Consideration of the problem of the devotional life of those who find it difficult to attend public worship regularly and to use the appointed means of grace, e.g. mothers of families.

(g) The promotion of an analysis, psychological, historical, and theological of the conditions and circumstances, both of origin and development, of particular traditions of Christian faith and worship.

(h) An examination of the existing situation in which some Churches regard the preaching of the Gospel as well as the eucharistic act as essential for worship, whereas others regard the Eucharist as by itself containing the essential elements of worship.

(i) A more detailed exploration, theological, metaphysical, and psychological, of *mystery* in relation to worship. If this enterprise recommends itself, we urge a proper co-operation with those expert in the psychological material relevant to our purpose.

127   N.B.—We stress the need to enlist the interest not only of liturgical experts, and of those responsible for the conduct of worship, but especially of members of the worshiping congregations.

V. INTERCOMMUNION

I. INTRODUCTION

A.

130   In the Report of the Second World Conference on Faith and Order at Edinburgh in 1937, the statement is made: "We regard sacramental intercommunion as a necessary part of any satisfactory church unity." The Continuation Committee felt the need of at once setting up a Commission to study the problems involved in the achievement of intercommunion, and made this one of the main subjects for consideration at the Lund Conference. During the past fifteen years, the Churches have been drawn closer together in worship, thought, and service. The urgency of making progress toward closer fellowship at the Lord's Table is very widely felt in all parts of the world.

131   There are those for whom the very word "Intercommunion" raises difficulties. In their view the observance of Holy Communion is an act of the Church as One Body. It cannot properly be celebrated as a joint act of bodies which in their church life and doctrine are separated from

each other. This is the view of the Orthodox Church. It seems well to make clear at the outset that so far as the Orthodox are concerned the question of intercommunion as ordinarily understood does not exist.

132 Our discussions have naturally been mainly concerned with the views of those Churches which are able to envisage sacramental fellowship without complete organic union. For almost all of these Churches the matter has become one of growing concern. The following considerations indicate the seriousness of the issues at stake:

133 (1) By joining together in the World Council of Churches, the Churches have taken a decisive step toward closer association. They have affirmed their will to stay together and to bear one another's burdens. This new mutual commitment raises ever more sharply the question of what justification remains for continuing in division at the Lord's Table.

134 (2) New factors in the present historical situation demand that any barriers to fellowship which are not based on fundamental divergences of faith and order should be removed as speedily as possible. We need only refer here to the new missionary opportunities in Asia and Africa, the tragic stress of persecution and war conditions, the new inter-Church agreements and unions in both East and West, and the increasing demand of Christian Youth to be set free from barriers to unity in fellowship and action.

135 (3) The ultimate urgency comes from our Lord's call to us. He calls His Church to lay open all its life to His transforming power. In their earthly pilgrimage, Christians are always under His judgment, and in the midst of their divisions live always toward the day of His final sifting of those who have in faith truly served Him and those who have not. Christ's followers stand under the imperative of His prayer that they all may be one. They are bound to work and pray to overcome whatever separates them from one another in the sacrament of Holy Communion.

136 There are some for whom these considerations have such weight that they find it difficult to brook any delay in the achievement of intercommunion. We are painfully aware that as long as we remain divided at the Lord's Table, we cannot fully enjoy and express the unity which has been given us in Christ. On the other hand, we recognise that non-theological factors may sometimes lead to the pre-

mature union of separated bodies of Christians. It is of the utmost importance that all unions find their basis in the teaching of Scripture and be tested by conformity to the Word of God. There should be no move toward intercommunion which would treat our differences superficially or would use intercommunion as a means of by-passing difficulties.

B.

137   During the years since the Edinburgh Conference we have become increasingly conscious of the depth and difficulty of the issues of faith and order which must be faced if closer unity at the Lord's Table is to be achieved. It is not a question merely of human pride and stubbornness, much as we confess that these are operative in all of us. The difficulties arise from profoundly held differences of conviction about the nature of the Church and of the sacraments. These cause grief and perplexity to us all. Their character and extent have already been examined in earlier sections of this report. The achievement of full sacramental fellowship depends, in part at least, upon fuller agreement in these matters.

138   For many of us the Open Services of Holy Communion held at Tambaram, Amsterdam, and Lund have been encouraging occasions of ecumenical fellowship in this central act of the Church's worship. Nevertheless, the fact that some of our number could not conscientiously participate in these services has demonstrated to all of us the painful nature of the problem. The prayerful self-searching in love which all of us have been forced to make on such occasions is, we believe, an earnest of the Lord's continual presence and of His ultimate purpose to make us one in Him.

139   We acknowledge, then, the complexity of the task which still lies before our Churches, but believe that we see more clearly the issues at stake and the need for continued thought and prayer together.

II. TERMINOLOGY

140   In the Edinburgh Report, the conviction was expressed that when the term "intercommunion" is used in discussion of church unity "its meaning should be clearly defined." The developments of recent years have made this essential, but the relationships which exist between Churches are so

117

varied that it is extremely difficult to find a terminology that is generally acceptable and can be easily understood by different traditions and in different languages.

141   The word "communion," or *koinonia*, denotes unity of fellowship in the whole life of the Church. The word "communion" has also come to be applied in a special sense by many Christians to the Lord's Supper.

142   For purposes of ecumenical discussion, and with respect to the relations between separated Churches, the following usages and definitions seem advisable. It is important to remember, however, that none of the relationships described below can be regarded as the fulfilment of that complete unity which we believe to be God's will for His Church. It should also be noted that the following categories are not all mutually exclusive. Thus, the agreement between the Old Catholic Church and certain Churches of the Anglican communion cited under (3) below could have been cited under (2).

143   (1) *Full Communion* (though the adjective need rarely be used): where Churches in doctrinal agreement, or of the same confessional family, allow communicant members freely to communicate at the altars of each, and where there is freedom of ministers to officiate sacramentally in either Church (i.e., *Intercelebration*) e.g., the Orthodox, Anglican, Lutheran, and Reformed (Presbyterian) "families" of Churches, respectively.

144   (2) *Intercommunion and Intercelebration:* where two Churches not of the same confessional family, by agreement allow communicant members freely to communicate at the altars of each, and where there is freedom of ministers to officiate sacramentally in either Church, e.g., Lutheran and Reformed Churches in France. N.B.—The relations at present existing between the Church of South India and the Church of England are a special case of this kind, involving certain specific limitations.

145   (3) *Intercommunion:* where two Churches, not of the same confessional family, by agreement allow communicant members freely to communicate at the altars of each, e.g., Churches of the Anglican communion and Old Catholics, Protestant Episcopal Church and Polish National Catholic Church in U.S.A. Subject to differences of language, etc., intercommunion in most cases would also involve intercelebration.

146   (4) *Open Communion:* where a Church on principle invites members of other Churches to receive communion when they are present at its communion services, e.g., the Methodist, Congregationalist, and most of the Reformed Churches.

147   (5) *Mutual Open Communion:* where two or more Churches on principle invite each other's members and the members are free to accept the invitation. This does not necessarily involve intercelebration.

148   (6) *Limited Open Communion* (Communion by Economy of Dispensation): the admission of members of other Churches not in full communion or intercommunion to the Sacrament in cases of emergency or in other special circumstances.

149   (7) *Closed Communion:* where a Church limits participation in the Lord's Supper to its own members.

III. THE ORDERING OF THE LORD'S TABLE

A.

150   (1) We are agreed that the Table is the Lord's and that He gives Himself to us in the sacrament of Holy Communion. When we are unable to share together in the Lord's Supper, the pain and scandal of our divisions is most severely felt because we seek the one Lord, and know that we should be able to partake as brethren in the family of God at one Table.

151   (2) We further agree that the responsibility for the due ordering of the Table in the name of Christ has been committed to the Church. She has to warn her members that if they "eat and drink unworthily, not discerning the Lord's Body," they bring themselves under judgment. Because of our divisions the exercise of this responsibility, in the formulation of regulations for admission to the Table, is carried out by the several Churches. In this administration each has a grave responsibility before God, particularly if it withholds the sacrament from any of God's people. Baptism, instruction, profession of faith, and some standard of Christian conduct are generally required. Thus the requirement of episcopal Confirmation on the part of some Churches is one way of discharging the Church's responsibility in this matter. Those Churches which practise Open Communion have their own requirements for participation;

119

the invitation extended is not to be interpreted as applying to the unbelieving or the unprepared.

152   (3) We are agreed in recognising the administration of the Lord's Supper in the divided Churches, when controlled by the words of institution, as real means of grace through which Christ gives Himself to those who in faith receive the appointed elements of bread and wine.

153   (4) The Churches have progressed toward unity in their understanding of the theological interpretation of the sacrament of the Lord's Supper, and we believe that agreement in this field is in fact greater than commonly appears. We have studied with satisfaction the statement of doctrine contained in the Report of the preparatory Commission on *Intercommunion* (pp. 29-30), and believe that the great majority of our Churches are able to accept it in this slightly amended form: This dominical sacrament of Christ's Body and Blood, controlled by the words of institution, with the use of the appointed elements of bread and wine, is: (a) a memorial of Christ's incarnation and earthly ministry, of His death and resurrection; (b) a sacrament in which He is truly present to give Himself to us, uniting us to Himself, to His eternal Sacrifice, and to one another; and (c) eschatologically, an anticipation of our fellowship with Christ in His eternal kingdom.

B.

154   We differ as to the right or responsibility of a Church to refuse admission to the Lord's Table to members of other Churches, or to restrain its own members from participating in the sacraments of another Church, on the grounds of divergence in faith or order.

155   (1) The majority of us, without for a moment losing sight of the ultimate goal of full unity, believe that there already exists among the members of the World Council of Churches such a fundamental unity as to justify, or indeed require, joint participation at the Lord's Table. Those who hold this view would express their position thus:

156   A valuable preparation for the fuller unity to which we look forward would be the extension of the practice of intercommunion between different Churches. This is borne out by the experience of the Churches in South India in the years leading up to the union of 1947. Intercommunion is not a substitute for reunion. It is not an end to itself. It

does not imply that all differences are resolved or have lost their significance. While intercommunion is, in many ways, illogical and anomalous, we ought to realize that the situation in which we all stand and with which we have to deal is itself highly anomalous. By membership together in the World Council of Churches we all recognize in each other's Churches "elements of the true Church"[4] and yet we are separated from each other. In advocating intercommunion, we do not mean that all the Churches here represented should at once declare themselves to have intercommunion with each other. Intercommunion must be agreed upon between two or more Churches as such, on the basis of a common life in Christ, sufficient to preclude any unreality in the practice of intercommunion. It might involve conditions, and even sacrifices, though not of principle. But we affirm that intercommunion, when thus agreed without sacrifice of principle, may properly and beneficially precede reunion. There will be no perfect solution of our problem until full visible unity. In the meantime, the extension of the practice of intercommunion, with all its difficulties, appears to be a valuable way forward.

157   Where there still cannot be any formal relationship of intercommunion, there should be an extension of the practice of open communion services on special occasions and in special circumstances.

158   (2) Others, without questioning the reality of our present unity, believe that fellowship in the Sacrament rightly exists only where there is fuller agreement in doctrine, a mutually acceptable ministry, or organic unity of church life.

159   Certain Lutheran Churches, maintaining that fellowship in the Lord's Supper depends upon the unity of the Church, and that such unity exists only where there is agreement in the proclamation of the Gospel, are unable to practise intercommunion where this would imply that the doctrine of the real presence of the Body and Blood of Jesus Christ in, with, and under the elements of bread and wine is false or unimportant. Many Anglicans, in accordance with the statement of the Lambeth Conference, 1930, would hold that "intercommunion should be the goal of, rather than a means to, the restoration of unity" (resolution 42)

[4]See To 12.

and that they should always in these matters so act as to bear witness to the principle that the proper minister of the Sacrament is a priest episcopally ordained.

160   It should be observed, however, that with the exception of the Greek Orthodox Church, no one of the member Churches of the World Council so strictly interprets its responsibility for the ordering of the Lord's Table as to deny the Sacrament to members of other Churches in cases of urgent need.

C.

161   All our Churches are profoundly concerned about the problems connected with intercommunion. Differences in practice and theology do not here correspond exactly with denominational or confessional boundaries. In certain Churches there is acute division of opinion on these issues. We have not been able to resolve the differences and tensions that exist among us. They will be found set out with great care and at greater length, and discussed from varying points of view, in the volume *Intercommunion*.[5] This volume deserves most careful attention and should receive earnest and sympathetic study by all our church authorities.

162   Our discussions together at Lund lead us to recommend that:

(1) All Churches should re-examine their ways of ordering and administering the Lord's Supper with a view to discovering whether there is or can be agreement with regard to the basic requirements from communicants. Greater thought and care on this matter by all Churches might well pave the way for closer agreement, and help toward relationships of intercommunion where these do not at present exist.

163   (2) All Churches should give attention to the relationship of their theology and practice of Baptism to their theology and practice of the Lord's Supper. Our attention has been drawn to the suggestion that "to refuse the Eucharist to those baptised into Christ Jesus and incorporated into His resurrection-body (i.e., the Church) amounts either to a denial of the transcendent reality of Holy Baptism or to attempted schism within the Body of

[5]*Intercommunion*, the Report of the Theological Commission appointed by the Continuation Committee of the World Conference on Faith and Order, ed. by Donald M. Baillie and John Marsh, 1952.

Christ."[6] We believe that this challenging statement might provide the starting point for further fruitful ecumenical discussion.

164   (3) Churches which require full doctrinal agreement prior to communion fellowship and Churches which require episcopal ordination as the test of a valid sacrament should carefully re-examine their practice in the light of exceptions which are already customary by way of Limited Open Communion, or Communion by Economy or Dispensation.

165   (4) Churches which practise Mutual Open Communion should seriously examine the objections to the practice urged on grounds both of doctrine and order. They should also ask themselves whether they could not and should not move toward a closer relationship of visible unity, in view of the relationship of the Sacrament to the wholeness of the Church.

166   In closing this section of our report, we cannot but express our deep disappointment and concern that there is not a larger measure of agreement among us.(We echo the view of the preparatory Commission on *Intercommunion* that "neither we nor the Churches from which we come have yet gone deeply enough into the penitence from which healing may arise."[7]

IV. Communion Services at Ecumenical Gatherings

167   The growth of the Ecumenical Movement has greatly sharpened in recent years the problem of communion services being held in the setting of conferences where Christians from a variety of Churches are gathered together for some days or weeks. Their life and worship together are not complete unless they can have the fellowship of the Lord's Table. In cases where all the Churches represented are in Full Communion or Intercommunion with each other (or are prepared to sanction an Open Communion on such occasions), there need be no difficulty; a single communion service can be arranged, at which a minister will celebrate according to the order of his own Church, and all can partake. But where these conditions do not exist there is a real problem, which has been felt acutely by many in recent years. We recognise that we are only at the begin-

[6]*Ibid.*, p. 339.
[7]*Ibid.*, p. 31.

ning of the consideration of this problem and do not yet realise all its implications.

168   It is to the Church of Christ that the sacrament of Holy Communion is entrusted, and wherever a minister celebrates, his action involves the implicit claim that he does so as a minister of the Church Universal. In the present state of division, however, although he is commissioned in the name of Christ, his authority is derived through one of the Churches only, and will perhaps not be acknowledged by all. A conference, gathered together in the name of Christ, even though it may be regarded as a temporary and local expression of the Church, does not claim the right to ordain or authorize its own ministry to celebrate the Sacrament. Consequently, when the members of such a group belong to Churches which are not in communion with each other (in any of the ways mentioned above), no one celebrant will be recognized by all as properly authorized to administer the Sacrament. When all members are not able to meet at the Lord's Table, no service which is held can be regarded as *the* communion service of the conference. For such difficult situations we wish to make the following recommendations:

RECOMMENDATIONS

169   (1) There should always be a united service of preparation for Holy Communion, with special emphasis on the note of penitence for our separation from each other.

170   (2) There should be opportunity for communion services at such times as will make it possible for every member of the conference to receive communion somewhere without violation of his own conscience or disloyalty to his church tradition. These should be held at different times.

171   (3) Though on the grounds already indicated there are some who object to open communion services, yet we believe there should be an opportunity of this kind for the many who desire such services and are free to partake. Such services should where possible be held on the invitation of the local church or churches which sanction such services.

172   (4) At conferences held at places remote from local churches, or in ecumenical institutions, similar arrangements may be made within the conference or community.

The celebrant in each case should be a minister, who will celebrate according to the order of his own Church, and issue such an invitation as he is authorized to give.

173 (5) It is important that those who cannot partake at a particular communion service should be invited to attend the service as worshippers, though they cannot receive communion. This has been found by many to be a means of real blessing of spiritual communion, and of deeper understanding and fellowship.

174 In making these recommendations we realize that they do not by any means solve the practical problem, which arises from the as yet unreconciled divergences in the doctrine of the Church. Doctrinal as well as practical issues must be further explored. We are agreed that this particular aspect of the problem of intercommunion should be very strongly driven home upon the conscience of the Churches and of the leaders of the Ecumenical Movement. In particular further careful study of the principles underlying procedure at ecumenical conferences and institutions should be undertaken by the Faith and Order Commission.

VI. WHERE DO WE STAND?

I.

175 We confess our faith in the One, Holy, Catholic and Apostolic Church which is God's gift for the salvation of the world. The saving acts of God in Christ brought the Church into being, and it persists in continuity in history by the power of the Word of God and the presence of the Holy Spirit.

176 The Church's vocation is to glorify God in adoration and in self-sacrificing service to mankind, bearing witness in its corporate life to God's redeeming grace in Jesus Christ, proclaiming the Good News to every creature, making disciples of all nations, and bringing Christ's commandments to communities as well as individuals.

177 We make these affirmations in our conviction of an underlying unity of life in Christ. Christ has made us His own and Christ is not divided. In seeking Him we find one another, and we humbly and gratefully acknowledge this unity as given of God. It enables us to face our divisions penitently, and under the continued guidance of the Holy

125

Spirit we resolve to seek new ways of approach to each other.

178 Discussion reveals serious differences, especially concerning the beliefs held by or within some of the Churches about the authority of the Church, its limits and the mode of its definition. The examination of these differences in the preparatory work of the Theological Commission and in the experience of personal encounter reveals an encouraging degree of common ground. We have made genuine progress and there is no reason for pessimism. Nevertheless we have now reached a point at which our divergences stubbornly resist easy solution.

179 Part of the difficulty is that the language which expresses our understanding of the faith is sometimes an inadequate means of communicating our convictions one to another. We may discover that some of this language embodies insights which in the divisions of the Church have become isolated from the wholeness of Christian Truth. Often particular emphases become restrictive bonds, from which denominational life is not easily freed. It is in ecumenical meeting that we are made aware of a wholeness that must both include and complete the faith and life of the separated members of God's Family. There we are faced with the dilemma of a proper confessional loyalty and obedience to the richer unity of the One Church to which Christ points us, of which through the Faith and Order movement we have caught a clearer vision.

II.

180 Conscious and deliberate theological work is always one important line of advance, as the Report of the Theological Commission on The Church states. Recent research in various fields throws new light on our disagreements. We suggest serious consideration of the following:

181 By the final revelation of God in Jesus Christ at a particular point in history, the Church lives, but it is within the continuous movement of history that it bears witness to this Gospel and applies it to human need. The thought forms and language through which the Church proclaims the one Gospel are therefore subject to the limitations and changes of history. But the nature of any given historical period is such that in no one age can the truth of God's revelation be given full expression. This does not mean

126

that the Church should subordinate its message to the relativities of history, for we believe that the revelation of God in Jesus Christ and the scriptural witness to it are unique and normative for all ages. The Church should seek to proclaim this truth in ever-new terms, but the language and thought-forms coined in history must be constantly corrected by the content of the Gospel. This is also true of those means by which the Churches have confessed their faith in decisive moments of their history. We must always make sure in contending for our distinctive convictions that we distinguish between the confession of the Truth to which we are committed and those expressions of it that were in part products of a particular age. If all denominations are prepared to do this in obedience to the Gospel alone, we may well come nearer to one another.

182   Furthermore, this work of interpretation of the Churches to each other and to the world takes place in an intellectual climate that has undergone far-reaching changes. Our understanding of the Scriptures to which the Reformers made their primary appeal has greatly advanced. Whereas this in itself has brought new problems, it has also given a new expression to the Biblical revelation in its greatness and transcendence. As examples we may cite developments in the study of Biblical estimates of man, Biblical forms of communication, and Biblical methods of interpretation. This Biblical study cuts across denominational lines and often provides a fresh starting-point for rethinking denominational relationships.

183   In addition scientific investigation of the physical universe has opened up new and vast horizons and most of our divisions antedate these great changes in our knowledge concerning man and the world in which he lives. This, clearly, does not affect our central convictions, but it has influenced the manner in which we present them to each other.

III.

184   The Gospel is always received by men living within certain particular circumstances—cultural, social, political, and economic. Within these circumstances Christians are called to embody and maintain their allegiance to God. The Church, constantly renewed and sustained by God's saving activity, lives in history and fulfils its mission under

127

the manifold pressures of man's finite and sinful life. It stands on the frontier between the Word and the world, constantly tempted by the motives of a society that seeks to organize and preserve itself apart from God. Many of our pre-suppositions and prejudices, usually unconscious and unavowed, are the outcome of worldly pride and self-assertion. Cultural conditions are sometimes treated as essential to the Gospel. National aims are on occasion identified with God's will. We have all received patterns of thought not only from the Gospel but also from the structure of society (e.g., we are influenced by conflicting conceptions of freedom and justice, equality and democracy). These conceptions sometimes colour our understanding of the Gospel and tend to divide us.

185   The importance of such influences upon our Churches cannot be denied. They have played a part in creating our divisions. They still play a part in maintaining these divisions. They inhibit our understanding of the message of salvation and seriously impede the fulfilment of our mission. Unless they are seriously tested as in the sight of God, they may involve us unawares in a dangerous complacency. The Churches must therefore examine those areas in which these influences are most productive of suspicion and even hostility among Christians. We meet such problems, for example, in the tension between Roman and non-Roman expressions of Catholicity, and where Churches are living and working in areas dominated by political systems which are sharply divided from one another.

186   When we seek to isolate the tensions due to these forces, we more readily locate the hidden factors in other people than we do in ourselves. We are slow to undertake the painful scrutiny of our own situation. If we are to deal courageously and adequately with these subtle forces, we must hear humbly and willingly what others say to us. God seeks to speak to each through the other and we may hear His voice only in the context of Christian brotherhood.

IV.

187   The Church in our time is experiencing anew the sense of crisis and urgency that marked the Apostolic Age. In a period when persecution is again a reality, the dividing walls between Christian groups become transparent, and a

128

new perspective on essentials and non-essentials brings a deeper unity to the people of God. When our obedience to the faith confronts the world with a strong Christian witness, suffering ceases to be a temporary emergency and becomes again a part of the normal experience of the Church. Christians who are complacent in their security are called not only to fellowship with their brethren under persecution, but to that humble self-examination which takes account of their own shortcomings and prepares them to bear whatever burdens God's will may lay upon them.

188   Members of the younger Churches have contributed to the understanding of our common task a distinctive emphasis which has greatly enriched our discussions. Under the constraint of the missionary imperative, they have discovered that the need of unity is fully understood only when related to the great task of evangelism. Their strong awareness of our fundamental oneness in Christ is due not merely to their relative immunity to the influences which produced and still maintain divisions among the older Churches, but also to their response to the demand for full obedience to the requirements of faithful witness and service. In their experience we can surely see the leading of the Holy Spirit. The miracle of this unity has disclosed to the older Churches the tragic extent to which their own witness has been impaired by their separation.

190   Furthermore we believe that all Christians are called to a deeper common participation in prayer and worship, in obedience, fellowship, and service. These, no less than theological discussion, are means whereby the unity of the Church in Christ is manifested and known.

191   The work of the Lund Conference and the nature of its true contribution to the life of the Body of Christ cannot be judged in the short perspective of a few days. The end of this Conference marks only the beginning of the ways in which its concern with the unsolved problems of the Church can, in the providence of God, extend its influence throughout the whole community of Christian people. In confronting the fundamental issues of Christian unity we have been working at a level far more profound than that at which our Churches originally discovered their more obvious agreements. This deeper sense of the tensions within the family of God has compelled us to face the crucial points of our disagreement. We have not resolved our differ-

ences nor brought forth before the world a simple method of achieving unity. Yet we have safeguards against complacency far more important in character. This Conference, by its very existence as well as by repeated emphasis, has called the Churches both to a deeper awareness of their common faith and to a more resolute effort to translate that faith into terms clearly visible in their common life. More perfect agreement waits upon a more adventurous courage and upon a more urgent effort of the will. We believe that "if any man will do his will, he shall know" what is God's purpose for His children.

192   In the task which lies ahead there is a part which every Christian can play. The insufficiency of our discipleship is due to the imperfection of our dedication to God's will. If our Churches have not risen to match the needs of the world with a clear demonstration of God's will and purpose, the cause lies partly in the apathy of so many who call themselves by Christ's name. When Christian people have humbly returned to the only springs of mercy and power, they will find that their feet are firmly set upon the path to that unity which God has designed for His people. Most earnestly therefore we summon all Christians to the duty of constantly renewed self-dedication to the will of God. And when we are ready humbly to receive what God is waiting to give us, we shall know that the greatest treasures of His Church are never of human achievement but always of divine grace.

193   *Note:* Each chapter of the foregoing Report was put to the Conference in plenary session and, after approved amendments had been made, was received *nemine contradicente*. On Thursday, August 28, the Chairman similarly put the Report as a whole to the vote of the Conference, which received it *nemine contradicente*, and commended it to the Churches for consideration.

The delegates representing the Orthodox Churches under the jurisdiction of the Ecumenical Patriarchate had taken part in the Conference in expounding the Orthodox view both in section meetings and in plenary sessions, but took no part in the voting upon the reception of the Report.

5.

EVANSTON

Second Assembly of
the World Council of Churches
September 15-31,1954

FAITH AND ORDER: OUR ONENESS IN CHRIST AND OUR DISUNITY AS CHURCHES

REPORT OF SECTION I

Received by the Assembly and commended to the Churches for study and appropriate action with the request that the Churches report the results of their study and action to the Central Committee.

"Christ in you, the hope of glory" (Col. 1:27).

INTRODUCTION

1 We speak as those who have met together in the World Council of Churches and have known for a fact that we have been given a "oneness in Christ," in spite of our "disunity as churches."

This oneness is no mere unity of sentiment. We become aware of it because it is given to us by God as the Holy Spirit reveals to us what Christ has done for us. In this report we have tried to make clearer what we believe about this given unity, in the prayer that if we, and the churches from which we come, strive earnestly to lay hold upon the meaning of that which is already given, the Spirit of God will open our eyes to still deeper understanding, and our hearts to still fuller enjoyment of the unity which is ours in Christ.

To that end:

First, we speak together with one mind and in accordance with the witness of the New Testament, of the oneness of the Church, as grounded in the whole work of Christ, as growth into the fulness of Christ, and as partially realized even in our present divided state.

Second, we speak of our disunity as churches as partaking of that disobedience over which Christ has won His victory, granting us even in our disunity some fore-taste of our ultimate unity in Him.

Third, we speak of some of the consequences for us, in the obedience of faith, as we meet together in His saving Name to beg Him to fulfil His unifying work in us.

I. Our Oneness in Christ

A. *Christ's Unifying Work*

2   The New Testament conceives of the unity of the Church, not as sociological, but as having its essential reality in Christ Himself and in His indissoluble unity with His people (Acts 9:4ff; I Cor. 12:12; Jn. 15:1f). Hence we must still ask Paul's question about division in the Church: "Is Christ divided?" (I Cor. 1:13), and assert with the Apostle the indestructible unity that belongs to the Church in Christ. Christ is the *one* Lord who represents and gathers to Himself the *many* of redeemed humanity, and it is therefore He alone who makes the many to be one in the Church (I Cor. 12:12; Eph. 1:10, 22; cf. Jn. 14:20; 17, 4ff.; I Cor. 6:16f).

3   The New Testament speaks in many ways of the relationship of Christ and His people to describe their unity in Him. The Church is many members in one body (I Cor. 12:12); the several members are subject to the one Lord as Head of the body (Eph. 1:22; 4:15; 5:23; Col. 1:18; 2:19); the Church is His bride, to be united to Him the bridegroom (Mk. 2:19; Rev. 19:7; cf. Mt. 22:2ff.; 25:10f.; Lk. 12:36; Eph. 1:22ff.) the faithful are His people (I Pet. 2:9f.; Col. 3:12; Rom. 11:2, 11f., 32); He is the new temple in whom true worship is offered (Jn. 2:ff.; cf. 4:21ff.) or the one building of which the believers constitute living stones (I Pet. 2:5; Eph. 2:20; cf. I Cor. 3:9); He is the vine, of which we are the branches (Jn. 15:1ff.), or the shepherd whose flock we are (Jn. 10:1ff.).

4   The New Testament thinks of the one life of the Church as deriving from the whole Person and work of Jesus Christ as Saviour and Lord. The Church's unity is grounded in His taking of our nature upon Him; in His own words and works by which the power and life of His kingdom were manifested; in His calling of men into the fellowship of His kingdom, and in the appointing of the Twelve to share in His messianic ministry and work; in His passion and death, where sin was finally conquered and the power of divisiveness defeated; in His resurrection, where He manifested the new man unto whom we all grow (Eph. 4:11ff.), in whom all human divisions are done away (Gal. 3:28); in His ascension and heavenly reign, by which all history is brought under His authority; in His outpouring of the Holy Spirit on the whole Church at Pentecost, which gives to each subsequent baptismal rite its deepest significance; and in His promise to come again as the triumphant and glorious king. Through the indwelling Spirit, the Comforter, who leads the Church into all truth, the unity of the Church even now is a foretaste of the fulness that is to be because it already is; therefore, the Church can work tirelessly and wait patiently and expectantly for the day when God shall sum up all things in Christ.

B. *The Oneness of the Church in Its Earthly Pilgrimage*

5   From the beginning the Church has been given an indissoluble unity in Christ, by reason of His self-indentification with His people. But the Church has never realized the fulness of that unity. From the beginning discord has marred the manifested unity of Christ's people (Lk. 22:24ff.; Mk. 10:35ff.). Thus we may speak of the oneness of the Church in its earthly pilgrimage as a growth from its unity, as given, to its unity, as fully manifested (Eph. 4:3, 13). In this way we may think of the Church as we are able to think of the individual believer, who may be said at one and the same time to be both a justified man and a sinner *(simul justus et peccator)*. In each Christian there is both the "new man" who has been created and yet must be put on daily (II Cor. 5:17) and also the "old man" who has been crucified with Christ and yet must be daily mortified (Col. 3:1-5). So the Church is already one in Christ, by virtue of His identification of Himself with it (Jn. 14:20; 15:1-5) and must become one in Christ, so as to manifest its true unity (Eph. 4:11-16) in the mortification of its divisions.

6   Christ of His love and grace has given His Church such gifts as it needs for its growth from unity to unity. The gifts are severally and together none other than Christ Himself, but each has its place and its function in the life of the Church as it strives to give obedience to its Lord. Christ has given His Spirit which is the bond of peace and love, and the guide to all truth. He has given apostles, prophets, evangelists, pastors, and teachers, that the unity of the body may be continually built up. He has given the Scriptures, the preaching of the Word, Baptism, and Eucharist by which the Church proclaims the forgiveness of sins and by which, in the power of the Holy Spirit, faith is quickened and nourished. He has given the Church the gift and power of prayer, by which the Church can plead both for its own unity and for the reconciliation of men to God and to one another. He has given it faith and hope and love, that in its own life a new divine unity shall be manifest in deeds, and that its service to the world shall be both a manifestation of unity and a summons to it.

7   The New Testament, therefore, testifies to us that the Church shares in the life both of this world and of that which is to come. Indeed the Church's life is encompassed by a "great cloud of witnesses" (Heb. 12:2)—and the Church must never forget that its citizenship is really there, in the heavenly places (Eph. 2: 6). Its responsibilities must be discharged in this present world, but it must never become conformed to the world.

8   Thus the fellowship (koinonia) that the members of the Church have is not simply human fellowship; it is fellowship with the Father and with His Son Jesus Christ through the Holy Spirit and fellowship with the saints, in the Church triumphant. In all the Church's life there is being manifested not simply the activity of mortal men, but the life of the whole Church, militant on earth, triumphant in heaven, as it has its unity in the one Lord of the Church, who is its life.

9   But all this cannot be asserted without understanding that the unity given to the Church in Christ, and gifts given to the Church to help and enable it to manifest its given unity, are not for the sake of the Church as a historical society, but for the sake of the world. The Church has

its being and its unity in the "Son of Man, who came not to be ministered unto, but to minister and to give his life a ransom for many." The being and unity of the Church belong to Christ and therefore to His mission, to His enduring the Cross for the joy that was set before Him. Christ wrought "one new man" for us all by His death, and it is by entering into His passion for the redemption of a sinful and divided world that the Church finds its unity in its crucified and risen Lord.

C. *The Oneness of the Church Partially Realized*

10 Jesus Christ has given to His Church the gift of Himself and thereby the means of corporate life. These gifts were given not solely to the Church of New Testament days, nor are they reserved for the Church in some ideal state which ought to exist but unhappily does not. We acknowledge these gifts as being in a real sense present possessions.

11 It would be ungrateful to a merciful God if we did not speak now of those gifts which assure us that the undivided Christ is present amongst us, pouring His life into us all, in spite of our divisions.

12 We all wait upon one Father, through the one Holy Spirit, praying that we may be ready to hear and obey when He takes of the things of Christ and shows them to us. We all read the Holy Scriptures and proclaim the gospel from them in the faith that the Word speaking through them draws us to Himself and into the apostolic faith. We all receive His gift of Baptism whereby, in faith, we are engrafted in Him even while we have not yet allowed it fully to unite us with each other. We all hear His command to "do this" and His word "This is my body . . . this is my blood" in the Sacrament of the Eucharist, even whilst our celebration of the Lord's Supper is not yet at one Table. We all receive a ministry of the Word and Sacraments, even whilst our ministries are not yet recognized by all to be imitators of Christ and to follow Him in moral obedience as we confess Him before men even though we are still unprofitable servants.

13 As we have come to know each other better in the World Council of Churches, we have come to appreciate the immense range of common practice and intention which we share. The *fact* of our common (though diverse) use of these gifts is a powerful evidence of our unity in Christ

135

and a powerful aid to reminding us that unity lies in His work and not in our own achievements. We have also discovered that the old confessional divisions are being crisscrossed by new lines of agreement and disagreement.

14   We give thanks to our Father for these evidences that our unity in Christ is a present reality, both in the World Council of Churches and in relation to other Christians whose fellowship we do not as yet fully enjoy. But the very fact that, in every case, our benefit from these mercies is marred by our separation from each other, compels us now to examine seriously how it is that our disunity as churches contradicts our unity in Christ.

II. Our Disunity as Churches

15   Only in the light of the Church in Christ can we understand the difference between diversity and division in the Church, and their relation to sin. There is diversity which is not sinful but good because it reflects both the diversities of gifts of the Spirit in the one body and diversities of creation by the one Creator. But when diversity disrupts the manifest unity of the body, then it changes its quality and becomes sinful division. It is sinful because it obscures from men the sufficiency of Christ's atonement, inasmuch as the gospel of reconciliation is denied in the very lives of those who proclaim it.

16   Divisions in the Church have been caused and are perpetuated, to a large degree, by sincere concern for the gospel. Some believe that others were departing from the God-given structure and faith of the Church by unwarrantable claims and unfounded doctrines. So came the schism between East and West. Some believed that God had called them to such reformation of the faith and order of the Church as would restore it to its primitive purity. They found their work could not be completed within the framework of Roman Catholicism; thus came the separate churches of the Reformation. Some believed that the faith must indeed be reformed but within the framework of ancient and historic episcopacy. So the Anglican and Old Catholic communions became separated both from Rome and from many of the Reformed churches. Some believed that the established churches of their day would not give free course to the Word of salvation. So the older free

136

churches and the Methodist connexion felt themselves forced to adopt independent church orders. Similar acts of conscientious obedience to the will of God have likewise resulted, even if unintended, in breaches of Christian fellowship in doctrine, sacraments, and order. God in His mercy has used such decisions to save souls, to build up communities who worship Him, and to preserve or recover aspects of His truth. All this we can and must say. But He has also given to us today a fresh awareness of the sin which characterizes the divided state which we have inherited. We shall never, in this life, escape from our sinfulness, but we can repent of sin when it is revealed to us. Even when we have done that which we thought it right to do, we must remember that we are culpably implicated in sin not wholly of our own making and cannot dissociate ourselves from the sin of division. Confession of oneness with Christ carries with it confession of solidarity with our brethren in sin.

17   We ask each other whether we do not sin when we deny the sole lordship of Christ over the Church by claiming the vineyard for our own, by possessing our "church" for ourselves, by regarding our theology, order, history, nationality, etc., as our own "valued treasures," thus involving ourselves more and more in the separation of sin. The point at which we are unable to renounce the things which divide us, because we believe that obedience to God Himself compels us to stand fast—this is the point at which we come together to ask for mercy and light. So what we believe to be our "faithfulness" must bring us together at the foot of the Cross. The Cross tells us that where the dividing power of sin was most manifest, there God has gained the victory. By the same Cross He is able to make all things to work together for good—even our divisions. By planting the Cross of Christ in the midst of our divisions we believe He will overrule all their sin and make them serve His purpose of unity.

18   Concretely, this means that when churches, in their actual historical situations, reach a point of readiness and a time of decision, then their witnessing may require obedience unto death. They may then have to be prepared to offer up some of their accustomed, inherited forms of life in uniting with other churches without complete certainty as to all that will emerge from the step of faith.

137

Otherwise, acts of apparent re-union might be merely acts of calculated self-aggrandizement and a betrayal of the true calling of the Church. But when churches have been ready in this sense "to die with Christ," they have found that He who raised Jesus from the dead is faithful and powerful still.

19 It is certain that the perfect unity of the Church will not be totally achieved until God sums up all things in Christ. But the New Testament affirms that this unity is already being realized within the present historical order. By the power of His resurrection, Christ has granted this grace to His Church even now, and the signs of His work are discernible to him who has eyes to see. In the upheavals of the present hour, Jesus Christ is gathering His people in a true community of faith and obedience without respect for existing divisions.

We must not assume that the divisions which now separate Christians from one another correspond to those which Christ brings about in times of tribulation. Still less can we think that they will coincide with the separation finally to be made by the Son of Man. In this eschatological perspective all our human divisions are provisional.

III. THE ACTION OF FAITH

20 Christ has made us one by breaking down walls of partition. We are nevertheless disunited as churches. How are we to act in the obedience of faith and hope in our one Lord?

21 At least we all ought to be united in thinking of our divisions with repentance: not the repentance we may expect of others, but that which *we* undertake ourselves— cost what it may—even when others are unwilling to follow. True repentance is the acknowledgement before God that we have sinned so as to be caught in the net of inexplicable evil and rendered unable to heal our divisions by ourselves. But we cannot in sincerity and truth repent of our various understandings of God's will for His Church, unless the Spirit Himself reveals that our understandings have been in error. Penitence cannot be hypocrisy. Neither can it truly be expressed without desire for forgiveness and amendment of life.

22 All of us as members of churches believe that we have been entrusted by God with certain elements of the one

138

Church of Christ which we cannot forfeit. But at least we in the World Council of Churches are committed to a fellowship in which we are ready to bring our convictions under scrutiny in the presence of our fellow Christians and in the presence of the living Christ. In common we seek to know the judgment of the Word of God upon these convictions as to any error which may be involved in them.

23   Together we suggest the following ways in which, being both united and divided, we all must seek to be obedient: (i) In thanking God joyfully for the actual oneness He has given us in the World Council of Churches, we must try to understand the theological implications of this ecumenical fact and to implement it in the concrete relations of neighbour churches. With the Lund Conference on Faith and Order, we ask the churches "whether they should not act together in all matters except those in which deep differences of conviction compel them to act separately." We do not minimize the deep differences separating some churches. Nor do we ignore the numerous attempts to unite churches and the achievements of such reunion. In the World Council of Churches we still "intend to stay together." But beyond that, as the Holy Spirit may guide us, we intend to unite. "The World Council of Churches is not . . . a Super-Church."[1] Hence we do not ask the World Council of Churches to initiate plans for union, but to keep providing occasions for honest encounter between divided Christians.

24   (ii) We must all listen together in the midst of our disunity to our one Lord speaking to us through Holy Scripture. This is a hard thing to do. We still struggle to comprehend the meaning and authority of Holy Scripture. Yet whenever we are prepared to undertake together the study of the Word of God and are resolved to be obedient to what we are told, we are on the way toward realizing the oneness of the Church in Christ in the actual state of our dividedness on earth. In this connection we need also to study together the significance of Christian tradition and our various traditions, as reflected in liturgy, preaching, and teaching.

25   (iii) We must consider frankly the influence of social and cultural difference upon the matters of faith and order which cause divisions, and also perceive how the events

[1]See To 3.

139

and developments of current history make disunity a most urgent question.

26   (iv) We must speak the truth in love with one another and practise that love towards those with whom we disagree (Eph. 4:15, 25). Sometimes this involves us in judgments which fellow Christians cannot recognize as being made in love. At other times, we are so conscious of both the sin and the cultural conditioning with which all our judgments are infected that we are tempted to be more tolerant than truth allows.

27   (v) We must learn afresh the implications of the one Baptism for our sharing in the one Eucharist. For some, but not for all, it follows that the churches can only be conformed to the dying and rising again in Christ, which both Sacraments set forth, if they renounce their eucharistic separateness. We must explore the deeper meaning of these two sacramental gifts of the Lord to His Church as they are rooted in His own redeeming work.[2]

28   (vi) We must seek to acknowledge beyond the bounds of our own church each ministry that preaches the gospel of reconciliation as a means whereby Christ performs His saving deeds. Especially need we to discover the meaning of the ministry of the laity for Christian unity.

29   (vii) We must bear witness together to the gospel of Him who has already overcome our sins and divisions and who graciously uses sinners as His servants. Our divided witness is a necessarily defective witness, and indeed a scandal in the face of the non-Christian world. We have scarcely begun to work out the essential connection between "mission" and "unity." Our Lord's own prayer (Jn. 17: 21.) must become our own, not only on our lips but in our lives.

30   (viii) The measure of our concern for unity is the degree to which we pray for it. We cannot expect God to give us unity unless we prepare ourselves to receive His gift by costly and purifying prayer. To pray *together* is to be drawn together. We urge, wherever possible, the observance of the Week of Prayer for Christian Unity, January 18-25 (or some other period suited to local conditions) as a public testimony to prayer as the road to unity.

31   We cannot discern all that will be disclosed to us when we look to Him who is the Head of the body and affirm

[2]See Lu 130-174.

140

our oneness in Him. We know that we shall be changed, but wherein we shall be changed we cannot know until, in the act of faith and self-denial, we are given to discern, through crucifixion and resurrection, the lineaments of the one true Body of Christ which our sinful dividedness obscures from ourselves and from the world. Rejoicing in the grace which has been bestowed upon us in His various gifts even in our sin and separateness, we here set our hope on our one Lord Jesus Christ, who comes to take control over our divided and broken estate and to heal it by His grace and power. At Amsterdam we said that we intend to stay together. He has kept us together. He has shown Himself again as our Hope. Emboldened by this Hope, we dedicate ourselves to God anew, that He may enable us to grow together.

The Declaration of the Orthodox Delegates Concerning Faith and Order

32   As delegates of the Orthodox Church participating at this Assembly of the World Council of Churches, we submit the following statement concerning the report of Section I. 1. We have studied the document with considerable interest. It falls into three parts: the first contains an able exposition of the New Testament doctrine of the Church. The organic character of the Church and her indissoluble unity with Christ are adequately stressed in the document. We feel that this at least provides fruitful ground for further theological elaboration. The second and third parts of the document deal with the divided state of Christendom and suggest practical steps toward union. It is our conviction that it does not follow logically and consistently from the first part and indeed if we do actually accept the New Testament doctrine of the Church we should come to quite different practical conclusions which have been familiar to us Orthodox for centuries. The whole approach to the problem of reunion is entirely unacceptable from the standpoint of the Orthodox Church.

33   2. The Orthodox conception of church unity implies a twofold agreement:

(a) The whole of the Christian Faith should be regarded as one indivisible unity. It is not enough to accept just certain particular doctrines, basic as they may be in themselves, e.g. that Christ is God and Saviour. It is compelling

141

that all doctrines as formulated by the Ecumenical Councils, as well as the totality of the teaching of the early, undivided Church, should be accepted. One cannot be satisfied with formulas which are isolated from the life and experience of the Church. They must be assessed and understood within the context of the Church's life. From the Orthodox viewpoint, re-union of Christendom with which the World Council of Churches is concerned can be achieved solely on the basis of the total, dogmatic Faith of the early, undivided Church without either subtraction or alteration. We cannot accept a rigid distinction between essential and non-essential doctrines, and there is no room for comprehensiveness in the Faith. On the other hand, the Orthodox Church cannot accept that the Holy Spirit speaks to us only through the Bible. The Holy Spirit abides and witnesses through the totality of the Church's life and experience. The Bible is given to us within the context of Apostolic Tradition in which in turn we possess the authentic interpretation and explication of the Word of God. Loyalty to Apostolic Tradition safeguards the reality and continuity of church unity.

34   (b) It is through the Apostolic Ministry that the mystery of Pentecost is perpetuated in the Church. The Episcopal Succession from the Apostles constitutes a historical reality in the life and structure of the Church and one of the presuppositions of her unity through the ages. The unity of the Church is preserved through the unity of the Episcopate. The Church is one Body whose historical continuity and unity is also safeguarded by the common faith arising spontaneously out of the fulness (*pleroma*) of the Church.

35   3. Thus when we are considering the problem of Church unity we cannot envisage it in any other way than as the complete restoration of the total faith and the total episcopal structure of the Church which is basic to the sacramental life of the Church. We would not pass judgment upon those of the separated communions. However, it is our conviction that in these communions certain basic elements are lacking which constitute the reality of the fulness of the Church. We believe that the return of the communions to the Faith of the ancient, united, and indivisible Church of the Seven Ecumenical Councils, namely to the pure and unchanged and common heritage of the forefathers of all separated Christians, shall alone produce

142

the desired reunion of all separated Christians. For, only the unity and the fellowship of Christians in a common Faith shall have as a necessary result their fellowship in the sacraments and their indissoluble unity in love, as members of one and the same Body of the one Church of Christ.

36   4. The "perfect unity" of Christians must not be interpreted exclusively as a realization at the Second Coming of Christ. We must acknowledge that even at the present age the Holy Spirit dwelling in the Church continues to breathe in the world, guiding all Christians to unity. The unity of the Church must not be understood only eschatologically, but as a present reality which is to receive its consummation in the Last Day.

37   5. It is suggested in the report of the section that the road which the Church must take in restoring unity is that of repentance. We recognize that there have been and there are imperfections and failures within the life and witness of Christian believers, but we reject the notion that the Church herself, being the Body of Christ and the repository of revealed Truth and the "whole operation of the Holy Spirit," could be affected by human sin. Therefore, we cannot speak of the repentance of the Church which is intrinsically holy and unerring. For, "Christ loved the Church and gave Himself for it, that He might sanctify it and cleanse it in the washing of water and the word, that He might present it to Himself as a glorious Church, not having spot or wrinkle or blemish or any such thing, but that it should be holy and without blemish." (Eph. 5:26-27).

Thus the Lord, the only Holy one, sanctified His Church for ever and ordained that her task be the "edification of the saints and the building of the body of Christ." Her holiness is not vitiated by the sins and failures of her members. They cannot in any way lessen or exhaust the inexhaustible holiness of the divine life which from the Head of the Church is diffused throughout all the body.

38   6. In conclusion, we are bound to declare our profound conviction that the Holy Orthodox Church alone has preserved in full and intact "the faith once delivered unto the saints." It is not because of our human merit, but because it pleases God to preserve "his treasure in earthen vessels, that the excellency of the power may be of God" (II Cor. 4: 7).

6.

NEW DELHI

*Third Assembly of
the World Council of Churches
November 18—December 6, 1961*

REPORT OF
THE SECTION ON UNITY

I. THE CHURCH'S UNITY

1   The love of the Father and the Son in the unity of the Holy Spirit is the source and goal of the unity which the triune God wills for all men and creation. We believe that we share in this unity in the Church of Jesus Christ, who is before all things and in whom all things hold together. In him alone, given by the Father to be Head of the Body, the Church has its true unity. The reality of this unity was manifest at Pentecost in the gift of the Holy Spirit, through whom we know in this present age the first fruits of that perfect union of the Son with his Father, which will be known in its fullness only when all things are consummated by Christ in his glory. The Lord who is bringing all things into full unity at the last is he who constrains us to seek the unity which he wills for his Church on earth here and now.

2   We believe that the unity which is both God's will and his gift to his Church is being made visible as all in each place who are baptized into Jesus Christ and confess him as Lord and Saviour are brought by the Holy Spirit into one fully committed fellowship, holding the one apostolic faith, preaching the one Gospel, breaking the one bread,

joining in common prayer, and having a corporate life reaching out in witness and service to all and who at the same time are united with the whole Christian fellowship in all places and all ages in such wise that ministry and members are accepted by all, and that all can act and speak together as occasion requires for the tasks to which God calls his people.

3   It is for such unity that we believe we must pray and work.

4   This brief description of our objective leaves many questions unanswered. We are not yet of a common mind on the interpretation and the means of achieving the goal we have described. We are clear that unity does not imply simple uniformity of organization, rite, or expression. We all confess that sinful self-will operates to keep us separated and that in our human ignorance we cannot discern clearly the lines of God's design for the future. But it is our firm hope that through the Holy Spirit God's will as it is witnessed to in Holy Scripture will be more and more disclosed to us and in us. The achievement of unity will involve nothing less than a death and rebirth of many forms of church life as we have known them. We believe that nothing less costly can finally suffice.

A Commentary upon This Picture of Unity

5   The foregoing paragraph must be understood as brief description of the sort of unity which would correspond to God's gift and our task. It is not intended as a definition of the Church and it does not presuppose any one particular doctrine of the Church. It is based upon a statement worked out by the Commission on Faith and Order, accepted by the Central Committee at St. Andrews in 1960 and sent to the member churches for consideration and comment.[1] The "Toronto Statement"[2] was a landmark in the World Council's thinking about itself and its relation to work for unity. Here we seek to carry that thought a stage further, not by dictating to the churches their conception of unity but by suggesting for further study an attempt to express more clearly the nature of our common goal. Christian unity has been the primary concern of the

[1]See p. 208.
[2]The Church, the Churches and the World Council of Churches, see pp. 167ff.

145

Faith and Order movement from the beginning, and the vision of the one Church has become the inspiration of our ecumenical endeavour. We re-affirm that we must go forward to seek the full implications of this vision. We present this statement in the hope that the churches both inside and outside the World Council of Churches will study it with care, and, should it be found inadequate, will formulate alternative statements, which more fully comprehend "both God's will and his gift."

In Him Alone . . . The Church Has its True Unity

6   It is in Jesus Christ, God's Son and our only Mediator, that we have union with God. It is he who has given this gift to us through his coming into our world. Unity is not of our making, but as we receive the grace of Jesus Christ we are one in him. We are called to bear witness to the gift of unity through offering our lives as sacrifices to his glory. The fact that we are living in division shows that we have not realized God's gift of unity and we acknowledge our disobedience before him. Our union with God is a mystery which passes our understanding and defeats our efforts to express it adequately. But as Christ has come visibly into this world and has redeemed men of flesh and blood, this union must find visible expression.

7   It is the living Christ who impels us to work and pray for a fuller manifestation among us of "the one hope which belongs to our calling." Thus the Faith and Order movement has found the focal point of its study in the person and work of Jesus Christ. Through its Commission on Christ and the Church it has sought to explore the biblical and historical witnesses to Christ, to determine what unity in the one Lord actually means. The unity which is given is the unity of the one Triune God from whom and through whom and to whom are all things. It is the unity which he gives to his people through his decision to dwell among them and to be their God. It is the unity which he gives to his people through the gift of his Son, who by his death and resurrection binds us together in him in his sonship to the one Father. It is the unity given to his people through his Spirit, and through all the gifts of the Spirit which enliven, edify, and empower the new humanity in Christ.

146

8   This statement uses the word "place" both in its primary sense of local neighbourhood and also, under modern conditions, of other areas in which Christians need to express unity in Christ. Thus being one in Christ means that unity among Christians must be found in each school where they study, in each factory or office where they work, and in each congregation where they worship, as well as between congregations. "Place" may further imply not only local communities but also wider geographical areas such as states, provinces or nations, and certainly refers to all Christian people in each place regardless of race and class.

Who Are Baptized into Christ

9   The mutual recognition of baptism, in one sense or another, has been a foundation stone in the ecumenical discussions of the present century. However, closer examination of the assumptions and implications of this fact invariably brings to light deep and wide divergences in theory and practice amongst the churches of the World Council of Churches. Much progress has already been made through the studies of Faith and Order in the understanding of the one baptism.[3] We would urge that these studies be widely circulated among the churches and that the churches in each place study the meaning of baptism together, and in the light of such studies seek to come to a deeper understanding of the baptism by which all have been sealed into the one Lord through their one faith and the gift of the Holy Spirit.

By the Holy Spirit

10   · The Church exists in time and place by the power of the Holy Spirit, who effects in her life all the elements that belong to her unity, witness, and service. He is the gift of the Father in the name of Jesus Christ to build up the Church, to lead her into the freedom and fellowship which belong to her peace and joy. For any achievement of a fuller unity than that now manifest, we are wholly dependent upon the Spirit's presence and governance.

[3]Conference on "The Nature of the Unity We Seek" at Oberlin, USA 1957, and in the Report *One Lord, One Baptism*, SCM Press and Augsburg Publishing House 1960.

Fully Committed Fellowship

11   The word "fellowship" *(koinonia)* has been chosen because it describes what the Church truly is. "Fellowship" clearly implies that the Church is not merely an institution or organization. It is a fellowship of those who are called together by the Holy Spirit and in baptism confess Christ as Lord and Saviour. They are thus "fully committed" to him and to one another. Such a fellowship means for those who participate in it nothing less than a renewed mind and spirit, a full participation in common praise and prayer, the shared realities of penitence and forgiveness, mutuality in suffering and joy, listening together to the same Gospel, responding in faith, obedience, and service, joining in the one mission of Christ in the world, a self-forgetting love for all for whom Christ died, and the reconciling grace which breaks down every wall of race, colour, caste, tribe, sex, class, and nation. Neither does this "fellowship" imply a rigid uniformity of structure, organization, or government. A lively variety marks corporate life in the one Body of one Spirit.

The One Apostolic Faith

12   The Holy Scriptures of the Old and New Testament witness to the apostolic faith. This is nothing else than those events which constitute God's call of a people to be his people. The heart of the Gospel *(Kerygma)* is Jesus Christ himself, his life and teaching, his death, resurrection, coming *(parousia)* and the justification and sanctification which he brings and offers to all men. The creeds of the Church witness to this apostolic faith. There are important studies now being undertaken of the relationship between Scripture and Tradition (which is Christian confession down the ages), and attention is drawn to the work of Faith and Order's Theological Commission on Tradition and Traditions.[1]

Preaching the One Gospel

13   Preaching proclaims anew to men in each generation the Gospel of our Lord Jesus Christ. In the faithful preaching of the Word the living Christ is present as our contemporary in every age; he grants us his grace, he comforts us and

[1] *The Old and the New in the Church,* SCM Press and Augsburg Publishing House 1961.

calls us to a renewed decision for him. In the human words of the preacher every new generation is confronted by the Christ as one who speaks to them where they actually are.

Breaking the One Bread

14   Nowhere are the divisions of our churches more clearly evident and painful than at the Lord's Table. But the Lord's Table is one, not many. In humility the churches must seek that one Table. We would urge the Commission on Faith and Order to continue study and consultation to help us identify and remove those barriers which now keep us from partaking together of the one bread and sharing the one cup.

Joining in Common Prayer

15   God is to be praised in every tongue and in the setting of every culture and age in an inexhaustible diversity of expression. Yet there are certain common factors in Christian worship such as adoration, penitence, intercession, petition, and thanksgiving which are grounded inevitable in the unique acts of God in Christ, discernible still in our divided traditions. As we learn more of each other, we shall more clearly discern this common heritage and express it more fully.

A Corporate Life Reaching Out

16   Mission and service belong to the whole Church. God calls the Church to go out into the world to witness and serve in word and deed to the one Lord Jesus Christ, who loved the world and gave himself for the world. In the fulfilment of our missionary obedience the call to unity is seen to be imperative, the vision of one Church proclaiming one Gospel to the whole world becomes more vivid and the experience and expression of our given unity more real. There is an inescapable relation between the fulfilment of the Church's missionary obligation and the recovery of her visible unity.

Ministry and Members Accepted by All

17   All agree that the whole Body is a royal priesthood. Yet one of the most serious barriers to unity is our diverse understanding of the nature of the ministry within the

149

corporate priesthood. All who have been engaged in church union negotiations testify to this fact. There are those, for example, who affirm the necessity of an episcopally ordained ministry in the apostolic succession while others deny that it is essential for the true Church. How can two such divergent positions on so important a matter be settled? In this, as in all matters relating to Christ's Church, it is upon the Holy Spirit we must rely. He will, if we faithfully search, reveal to us the ways in which we can have a ministry accepted by all. Here biblical, theological, and historical studies must be continued to seek to lay before the churches that which is necessary to have a true ministry according to God's Word. The mutual acceptance of members though not so formidable an obstacle as mutual recognition of ministries, still raises problems for some communions. The achievement of a ministry accepted by all would largely resolve the issues involved in the mutual recognition of members.

In All Places and All Ages

18   Every church and every Christian belongs to Christ. Because we belong to him, we are bound through him to the Church and the Christians in all places and all ages. Those who are united in each place are at the same time one with believers in all places. As members of the one Body they share both in each other's joys and sufferings. The Church as a universal fellowship means also that we are part of the people of God of all ages, and as such are one with Abraham, Isaac, and Jacob, and all their descendants in the faith until the end of the age. Work for unity in Christ is continually attacked by all the evil forces which fear the light of truth and holiness and obscure our own vision also. We now see our unity only darkly, but we know that then we shall see it clearly when we see him face to face. But it is also our hope which gives us courage to expose our differences and our divisions and call upon God to reveal to us even now that which has hitherto been hidden from our eyes. We pray, with the praying Christ, that *all* may be one. To this end we must work while it is day.

II. SOME IMPLICATIONS TO CONSIDER

19   If we accept this picture of the unity for which we must pray and work, it has implications for the life of our churches as lived at the local level, as confessions, and as we meet each other in ecumenical fellowship. If we shirk these implications, we come under judgment for turning away from the light that God has given us. So we ask our churches to consider seriously what those implications may be.

A. IMPLICATIONS FOR LOCAL CHURCH LIFE

20   The place where the development of the common life in Christ is most clearly tested is in the local situation, where believers live and work. There the achievements and the frustrations are most deeply felt: but there too the challenge is most often avoided. It is where we live and work together daily that our Lord's own test is most clearly imposed, "by this shall all men know that ye are my disciples, if ye have love one to another." Before and beneath all outward expression is the commandment to love one another as he has loved us. As soon as we begin to obey this command, we can ignore each other no longer and we shall actively seek the means of giving expression to that love. The Lund Conference on Faith and Order in 1952 put out this challenge in the form of suggesting that Christians ought always to seek to do together everything which conscience did not compel them to do separately.[5] Loyalty to conscience takes different forms in different traditions. In some churches, the rules of corporate discipline make very clear the limits of corporate action; in others there is a far greater area of free manoeuvre. But all of us must confess that, in the life of our churches at the local level, we are still far from being together in all those ways in which, with a good conscience, we might be. It will be through daily obedience in the paths that are already open to us that our eyes will be enlightened to the fuller vision of our life together. The disclosure of the goal is inseparable from the faithful walking in the way in which he leads us.

21   (a) There is need for an increase in opportunities of growing together as local churches; through common worship, Bible study groups, prayer cells, joint visitation, com-

[5]See Lu 3.

mon witness in our communities. Locally as in the whole ecumenical movement we should be especially ready in Christian love to seek out and to establish fellowship with those traditions and minorities to which we are not now related. Even where we are compelled to remain separate at present in central aspects of the life of our congregations there is considerable freedom from developing areas of common worship, witness, and service in homes and communities.

22 (b) Ordinary social life already brings men together into various associations—academic, professional, industrial, political, etc. Within these forms of unity there is need for a Christian unity of those who may learn from each other how to bear their witness in those settings. Ecumenical thought in the calling of the laity needs to be shared in groups of this kind and it has its own bearing on church unity, for denominational divisions are often found to be quite irrelevant on this frontier. What is the bearing of that discovery upon our inherited divisions?

23 (c) Sometimes Christians will find themselves in associations of this kind in situations where their witness will involve sharp conflict, and they may reach a point where they have to break with the association. Wherever such conflicts arise, Christians are called to give their witness to a true expression of unity.

24 (d) Since much of this lay witness cuts across denominational lines, it clearly calls for united planning and execution as men and women seek in a common discipline under Christ to express his Lordship over all life, drawing their local churches together in the process.

25 Our division at the Lord's Table may be most acutely felt at the local level, especially if Christians of separated church traditions are truly meeting each other in common obedience to Christ. Where they are content virtually to ignore each other as Christians, or where the ecclesiastical traditions raise no difficulty, the problem may not be felt. But this "scandal" of eucharistic division appears at every one of the three levels we are considering. Since it is at the local level that it comes home most persistently, if it is seen at all, this is the point at which briefly to consider what the problem is, for there is no point at which we more completely fail to understand each other.

26 For some Christians, the Lord's own command "Do this"

152

is an imperative which overrides all our divisions. If Holy Communion is the sovereign means of grace for the forgiveness and conquest of sin, then that is true of the sin of division as well. Thus it is intolerable and incomprehensible that a common love of God should not be expressed and deepened by common participation in the Holy Communion which he offers.

27   For some Christians, the essence of the Christian life is incorporation into the Body of Christ realized as fellowship in an organic and transcendent unity of faith, life, and love made visible in a pattern of ministry and sacraments which is indivisible. Then it is intolerable and incomprehensible that those who do not share the organic life should expect to share in its eucharistic expression.

28   For neither view can there be any final peace so long as others who are known to be in Christ are not with us at the Holy Communion. But there are serious and deeply felt differences about how we should behave in our present recognition that God wills a unity which we do not manifest.

29   Although the problem may be most acutely felt at the local level, it is not at this level that it can find any general solution. Local churches may rightly ask, however, that confessional convictions be made clear amongst them if they are to be saved from uncomprehending suffering. In certain places groups of Christians have entered into intercommunion with full knowledge of the gravity of the issue involved. In these instances there has been, if not ecclesiastical approval, at least the withholding of disapproval. None of us can ignore the issues which such action raises. The Table is the Lord's gift before it is our blessing. We must therefore ask whether there are situations, e.g. during unity negotions, when intercommunion is possible even before full union is achieved, and all must feel with renewed intensity the agony of broken communion at the one Table of the Lord.

30   In the WCC we commit ourselves, in our local churches also, to an abiding concern for each other. In staying together we have discovered more and more that Christ is present among those to whom we cannot, on the grounds of our differing convictions, grant the full meaning of the word "church." If Christ is present with them, is he not calling us in ways we cannot yet clearly discern, to move

153

out towards him in order that we may receive our full unity with him and with his people? When the real Christian encounter takes place locally, we are forced to face these vital questions. This self-examination is always difficult; for we cannot and must not surrender those truths and ways of church life which we believe are God's will for his Church, and which the others do not yet accept. At the same time, we cannot and should not refuse to move out to Christ whose presence we recognize in the life of the others.

31   In this situation are we not constrained by the love of God to exert pressure on the limits of our own inherited traditions, recognizing the theological necessity of what we may call "responsible risk"? We emphasize the word *responsible,* for such actions must be taken with sincere respect for our confessional position and with the full attempt to explore with the Christian communion to which we belong the meaning of what we are doing. Clearly also, the responsible risk will be different according to our different convictions. Nevertheless, unless there is this preparedness to seek for responsible ways of breaking through to fresh understandings, we cannot hope to be shown the way to that growing unity which we know to be God's will for us. Responsible use of local situations to explore such possibilities is a challenge in every place.

B. Implications for the Life of our Confessions

32   When we turn to consider the implications of a commonly accepted picture of our goal for our life as confessions or "denominations," the first point to be made is the diversity in our understanding of what is meant by confession or denomination. Obviously such understanding is related to our conception of the Church itself. For some, as for the Orthodox, there can be no simple distinction between "Church" and "confession" for the Church itself is understood as essentially undivided.[6] Others would speak more readily in terms of "interior schism" or "divisions" *within* the Church. But for the practical purposes of what follows, we agree that when we speak of confessions and denominations, we simply acknowledge the fact that we recognize the same Christ through a variety of corporate traditions,

[6] *Cf.* the contribution from the Orthodox members in the minutes of the Unity Section.

of long or short history and more or less clearly defined, but within each of them certain crucial elements are always preserved. Gospel and faith, baptism, eucharist and doxology, witness and service in our common life in the Body of Christ are all involved. We concentrate on the problems of (1) a doctrinal basis of unity, (2) baptism and unity, (3) eucharistic fellowship, or lack of it, (4) common action in witness and service, as this affects or is affected by our divided state. It is all too plain that our present answers are not fully adequate—yet no more adequate answers can be given until the churches themselves become more generally and vividly concerned with providing them.

1. Doctrinal agreement

33   In our consideration of next steps towards an agreed doctrinal basis for the unity we seek, two useful distinctions may be made—that intellectual formulations of faith are not to be identified with faith itself, and that *koinonia* in Christ is more nearly the precondition of "sound doctrine" than *vice versa*. The primary basis of this *koinonia* is the apostolic testimony in the Holy Scriptures and "the hearing of faith." Yet this primary biblical revelation was given to and through the apostolic Church and has continued to be witnessed to by our common historic creeds, specifically the Apostles' Creed and the Nicaeo-Constantinopolitan Creed.[7] There is, as it were, an "ecumenicity in time" which may be realized by serious attention both to the ancient witnesses and also to the gifts of light and truth given by the Spirit in various ages and traditions in the history of the people of God. "The one apostolic faith," referred to in Part I of this report, is, first and last, faith in Christ as Lord and Saviour to the glory of God the Father. An obvious practical corollary of this understanding is the recommendation that a next step towards unity, at the denominational level, would be a fresh consideration of our various doctrinal bases, in the light of the primacy of Scripture and its safeguarding in the Church by the Holy Spirit.

2. Baptism and unity

34   Our ecumenical fellowship is essentially based upon the fact that we all want to be obedient to God's commandment

[7]*Cf.* the agreement on doctrinal unity in the Report of the First World Conference on Faith and Order (Lausanne, 1927), the doctrinal basis of the Church of South India and "Agreed Statements" from the C.S.I. Lutheran Theological Conversations, 1948-1959 (Madras, 1960).

in being baptized "into the body" (I Cor. 12:13). Our failure to share in the one Table of the Lord, to live and act as one visible and united body is an obvious contradiction of the baptismal gift that we all claim to possess. This contradiction can be explained in some cases by unjustified rationalizations and must therefore be overcome. In other cases, it reflects an obvious lack of agreement as to the true nature of the fellowship into which baptism introduces us.

35 Mutual recognition of baptism (although it goes far) is not in itself a direct means of unity forthwith. This means that we must place our conceptions of baptism in a dynamic, forward-looking perspective and ask ourselves: Where does our baptism lead us? We all agree that baptism is both God's gift and human commitment, and that it supposes a growth into the "measure of stature of the fulness of Christ" (Eph. 4:13). By this growth the baptized believers can even now visibly manifest to the world the new race of a redeemed mankind. Common witness to our churches, to the world, to those who have not yet heard the Gospel and to those who refuse it, is our common responsibility here and now. Fellowship in witness and service may help us to discover the meaning of God's gift to all the members of his people.

36 Much fruitful thought is being given, especially in Faith and Order studies, to the deeper meanings of baptism into Christ.[8] Every such examination sheds some new light on a tangled issue. It is important that disagreement as to the meanings and modes of baptism does not now entail outright denial or non-recognition of non-approved baptism. Even more important is the wide agreement that the initiative in baptism is from God by his Holy Spirit and that the baptized person's appropriate response must be expressed in the entirety of the life of faith. Such an understanding of baptism would suggest to those churches which practise infant baptism that this entails a more serious enterprise of Christian nurture than is often the case—and, to those churches that practise "believers' baptism," that they should reconsider the place of infants and children in the household of faith. Baptism recognizes God's claim on us as his children. It marks out a person's "place" in the Family, so that

[8]Cf. One Lord, One Baptism, and Faith and Order Commission Minutes, Faith and Order Paper No. 31, 1960.

even if that person does not "take his place," it is there for him, awaiting his response to be a faithful soldier of Christ in the Church militant.

3. *Eucharistic unity and division*

37 We have already spoken of the deeply felt differences which centre in the word "intercommunion." A main responsibility for deepening understanding rests with those who are called to work and speak on behalf of their confessions as such. The present impasse presses the churches to re-examine all possible next steps that might be discovered, at any and all levels of their denominational life. Wherever existing convictions allow for more direct progress towards intercommunion between churches, it should be made without waiting for consensus and common action in the ecumenical movement as a whole. Moreover, if we reversed the usual order of discussion and focussed on eucharistic action—what God does and calls us to do at the Lord's Table—rather than (first of all) on eucharistic administration—i.e., the problem of valid ministry—we might find a clearer way to the heart of an adequate sacramental doctrine. As the matter stands at present, we have a major problem of interpreting to our people the grounds (biblical, traditional, etc.) of our widely varying practices —some of which seem to make intercommunion "too easy" and others "too hard." There is value in divided Christians experiencing the agony of non-communicating Eucharists —but there is an equal need to reassure the excluded that the agony is as great for the excluding. We must meet, in a responsible fashion, the rising tide of impatience amongst many people, and indeed among many others, for more prompt and certain progress toward mutual understanding in this most central and vital experience of Christian worship and witness. The urgency of finding a way to break through the present impasse on the question of intercommunion makes it imperative that denominations and confessions undertake a new examination of their eucharistic doctrines and liturgies in the light of all these new factors introduced by the ecumenical situation.

4. *Common action*

38 We have said that one outcome of such unity as we have envisaged would be the enabling of Christians to "speak

157

and act together as occasion requires in the tasks to which God calls the Church." We see two spheres of Christian action which call for unity for their best effect and which promote unity by their very undertaking. The first is in the area of Christian ethics and discipline—especially in the face of the demoralization of modern culture and the increasing importance of divided churches uniting in effective action. The second is in the varied field of Christian education—including the enlistment as well as the training of ordinands with proper gifts and grace. There is, of course, a sense in which this is a peculiar prerogative of each autonomous church. Yet surely the magnitude and scope of the problem as it now faces us, calls for effective, ecumenical action. Such action would itself be a means toward greater unity.

C. Implications for the Ecumenical Movement

39   As we have participated in intensified efforts to clarify the nature of the unity which we seek to manifest, four questions have commanded our attention regarding our fellowship together, especially in the ecumenical movement, and, more particularly, in our mutual commitment in the World Council of Churches.

1. *What are the proper functions and limits of the WCC in regard to unity among its member churches?*

40   (a) Our deepest responsibility in the ecumenical movement is faithful prayer for the unity of Christ's Church as and when he wills it. Faith and Order has long sought to encourage such prayer as it is focussed in the Week of Prayer for Christian Unity. We give thanks to God that recent years have witnessed a steadily widening observance of this Week throughout the world. But there is also need to think more deeply about the nature of the unity we pray, including the part which the ecumenical movement itself can play in developing a common understanding.

41   (b) It is agreed that the WCC must not attempt to violate the autonomy of any member church. Neither may the Council make official pronouncements on unity which contravene the recognized doctrines of member churches, nor attempt to impose any one conception of unity.

42   (c) In faithfulness to its constitutional function of proclaiming the oneness of the Church, the Council should

158

do all within the limits of its competence to enable the churches to perceive the meaning of unity and to realize it more fully. All the work of the Council has general relevance to this purpose. But the present and projected programme of the Commission on Faith and Order[9] is of particular importance. We mention only a few of these plans and suggest some others.

43 (d) The educative function of the Council is indispensable and needs extension. Most members of churches know little of the beliefs and practices of churches other than those of their own communion or tradition. All kinds of ecumenical conferences thus have value. There is still need for good literature to further ecumenical education. Many helpful publications are issued by the World Council from its headquarters, but in themselves they can only be capable of a very limited circulation in comparison with the size of our constituency as a whole. The general membership of the churches can only be reached if every member church uses its own organs of communication to the full.

44 (e) A certain kind of *consultative* assistance can be given by the Council to churches which are engaged in unity conversations. The Commission on Faith and Order has already begun to render such service, though only, of course, upon the request of churches concerned, by sending persons of exceptional knowledge and experience to meet the church members who are responsible for negotiating union.

45 (f) The Council's Faith and Order Commission has also convened several consultations on church union with representatives from nearly all countries and churches where union negotiations are in progress. And it has been publishing regularly a survey of such developments, as well as distributing the relevant documents. We trust that this will continue.

46 (g) Perhaps the time has now come for the Council to undertake a new service. Although church union negotiations are continuing to arise at a rapid pace in various lands, and we rejoice that this is so, it is not always immediately clear how each of these has important implications for many churches within the Council's fellowship. For example, if churches of two or more communions in a certain country make progress towards union, this has

[9]As set forth in the Report on the Future of Faith and Order (see p. 167ff).

159

relevance for churches of those same communions in other lands. Now, the Council is already accustomed to sending general statements of unity to the churches for their study and consideration. But could it not also address direct questions to particular churches, asking them on behalf of all the Council's churches to state what reactions they have to specific union negotiations in which their own communions are involved? This would both stimulate the interest of these churches in the obligation to manifest the unity of Christ's Church, and also provide useful information for the good of all. It would not infringe upon any church's inherent autonomy, but serve as a reminder that here too we are all "members one of another." We also raise the question as to whether, with due regard for freedom of faith and conscience, the good offices of the Council should be used to help in breaking deadlocks which sometimes arise as a result of church union negotiations and lead to the possibility of further schism.

47   (h) In pursuing its studies in the realm of faith and order, the Council may now be ready to make penetrating inquiries into the way in which the very structures of the many churches tend to impede efforts by those churches to manifest greater unity. This has been initiated already through the important study on "Institutionalism,"[10] the results of which we expect to see soon. But still more remains to be done in this field of studies on unity.

48   (i) Finally, we are persuaded that the time is ripe for a fresh general study, among the member churches, of the conciliar process in the Church of the early centuries. This would be an extension and application of the significant inquiry already begun by the Theological Commission on Tradition and Traditions.[11] This would call attention not only to the results in doctrine, discipline, and liturgy, but also to the processes by which they were achieved.

2. *How does current thinking on unity affect our understanding of the nature of the World Council of Churches itself?*

49   Having stood the test of a decade of discussion and criticism, the Toronto Statement still best expresses our understanding of the Council's nature. It could also be

[10]See *The Old and the New in the Church*, SCM Press and Augsburg Press, 1961.
[11]*Ibid.*

fruitfully studied as illuminating the nature of national and regional councils. However, the probing studies and the prompting developments of these ten years keep driving us to seek further clarification. Mere insistence upon deeper study will not guarantee fresh insight. We are learning what the Council is by *living* together with it; and so it shall be. Nevertheless, the need for careful reflection on the theological meaning of our new life in the Council continues to be unfulfilled.

50   At least we are able to say that the World Council is not something wholly other than the member churches. It is the churches in continuing council. It is not over or apart from the churches but next to them at all times. We should speak of the Council as "we" rather than "it" or "they." Furthermore, many Christians are now aware that the Council is in some new and unprecedented sense an instrument of the Holy Spirit for the effecting of God's will for the whole Church, and through the Church for the world. What bearing has this upon our conception of the Church's unity?

3. *How may world confessional bodies contribute to the ecumenical movement and the unity of the churches?*

51   Most of these organizations existed many years before the founding of the World Council. Their purpose is not only to clarify and strengthen confessional understanding and loyalty but to serve responsibly in the wider ecumenical movement. Their contributions to the whole movement are well known and much appreciated. Their leaders are, for the most part, leaders in the World Council of Churches also. But opinion today is divided over the effects of their existence and work upon the participation of their churches in the movement for unity and upon the course which they ought to take in the future.

52   Some hold that a deepening understanding of the doctrines and traditions of the various confessions will in the long run enhance the possibilities of unity in the truth, even though for the present it may seem to restrain the churches from joining in full fellowship with one another. It is possible that unity could be further advanced by more frequent conversation between leaders of the confessions at the level of world organization. Already there are theo-

161

logical conversations in process between the Presbyterians and, respectively, the Lutherans and Congregationalists.

53   A contrary view is held by those who see the world confessional bodies as a threat to wider unity in particular areas, a view which some Asian and African Christians have often expressed with vigour.

54   Probably the critical question is whether or not the leaders of confessional bodies agree with the emphasis we have already made upon the centrality of the unity of all Christians *in each place*, which must, of course, always seek to be a "unity in the truth." If they agree, they will not consider the union of one of their churches as a loss, but as a gain for the whole Church. And a service can be rendered to such churches if the confessional bodies assist them in the responsible study of all issues which are involved in a proposed union.

4. Is the World Council now able to find new light on the problem of intercommunion?

55   We call the attention of the churches to the reports of the Youth Assembly at Lausanne, 1960, the Bossey Consultation of March, 1961, and the Pre-Assembly Youth Conference at New Delhi.[12] In all of these the tones of anguish and urgency are dominant, and the proposals for the adjustment of church policies on intercommunion are specific. The problem of Holy Communion at ecumenical conferences received particular study in these reports. But the following points may be noted:

56   (a) This is not a division between generations but *between and within the churches*. There are numerous older Christians whose sense of anguish and urgency is not exceeded by the younger. It is a problem for all churches and their members, and no one has excuse for apathy or resignation towards it as we meet in ecumenical gatherings.

57   (b) Surely a reconsideration of the policy laid down at Lund 1952 is now needed. But it is not yet clear that the proposals made at Bossey in 1961 provide a better agreement. Time for more reflection upon this might well be available before the Fourth World Conference on Faith and Order in 1963, when we hope that further consideration of this question will be undertaken.

[12]*Youth* No. 2, Oct. 1960, pp 79 ff. (Findings, Lausanne Youth Assembly); *Ecumenical Review*, vol. XIII no. 3, April, 1961 (report of Bossey Consultation).

58   In this concern for unity at every level of church life, we are mindful that the unity we seek is not for its own sake nor even for our sake. It is for our Lord's sake and for that of the world which he died to save. Unity is inseparable from renewal in holiness and truth, to God's glory. We offer this report to the churches in the prayer that it may contribute to deeper unity in our witness and service in the name of Jesus Christ, the Light of the World.

II
Statements Received
by the Central Committee
of the World Council of Churches

1.

THE CHURCH, THE CHURCHES AND THE WORLD COUNCIL OF CHURCHES

The Ecclesiological Significance of the World Council of Churches

Received by the Central Committee at Toronto in 1950 and commended for study and comment in the Churches

I. INTRODUCTION

1 The first Assembly at Amsterdam adopted a resolution on "the authority of the Council" which read:

"The World Council of Churches is composed of Churches which acknowledge Jesus Christ as God and Saviour. They find their unity in Him. They do not have to create their unity; it is the gift of God. But they know that it is their duty to make common cause in the search for the expression of that unity in work and in life. The Council desires to serve the Churches which are its constituent members as an instrument whereby they may bear witness together to their common allegiance to Jesus Christ, and cooperate in matters requiring united action. But the Council is far from desiring to usurp any of the functions which already belong to its constituent Churches, or to control them, or to legislate for them, and indeed is prevented by its constitution from doing so. Moreover, while earnestly seeking fellowship in thought and action for all its members, the Council disavows any thought of becoming a single unified church structure independent of the Churches which have joined in constituting the Council, or a structure dominated by a centralised administrative authority.

"The purpose of the Council is to express its unity in another way. Unity arises out of the love of God in Jesus Christ, which, binding the constituent Churches to Him, binds them to one another. It is the earnest desire of the Council that the Churches may be bound closer to Christ and therefore closer to one another. In the bond of His love, they will desire continually to pray for one another and to strengthen one another, in worship and in witness, bearing one another's burdens and so fulfilling the law of Christ."[1]

This statement authoritatively answered some of the questions which had arisen about the nature of the Council. But it is clear that other questions are now arising and some attempt to answer them must be made, especially in the face of a number of false or inadequate conceptions of the Council which are being presented.

II. THE NEED FOR FURTHER STATEMENT

2   The World Council of Churches represents a new and unprecedented approach to the problem of inter-Church relationships. Its purpose and nature can be easily misunderstood. So it is salutary that we should state more clearly and definitely what the World Council is and what it is not.

This more precise definition involves certain difficulties. It is not for nothing that the Churches themselves have refrained from giving detailed and precise definitions of the nature of the Church. If this is true of them, it is not to be expected that the World Council can easily achieve a definition which has to take account of all the various ecclesiologies of its member Churches. The World Council deals in a provisional way with divisions between existing Churches, which ought not to be, because they contradict the very nature of the Church. A situation such as this cannot be met in terms of well-established precedents. The main problem is how one can formulate the ecclesiological

[1] Amsterdam, Report of Committee II (Policy). *Cf.* Official Report, ed. by W. A. Visser't Hooft, p. 127.

implications of a body in which so many different conceptions of the Church are represented, without using the categories or language of one particular conception of the Church.

In order to clarify the notion of the World Council of Churches it will be best to begin by a series of negations so as to do away at the outset with certain misunderstandings which may easily arise or have already arisen, because of the newness and unprecedented character of the underlying conception.

III. WHAT THE WORLD COUNCIL OF CHURCHES IS NOT

3   1) *The World Council of Churches is not and must never become a Super-Church*

It is not a Super-Church. It is not the World Church. It is not the Una Sancta of which the Creeds speak. This misunderstanding arises again and again although it has been denied as clearly as possible in official pronouncements of the Council. It is based on complete ignorance of the real situation within the Council. For if the Council should in any way violate its own constitutional principle, that it cannot legislate or act for its member Churches, it would cease to maintain the support of its membership.

In speaking of "member Churches," we repeat a phrase from the Constitution of the World Council of Churches; but membership in the Council does not in any sense mean that the Churches belong to a body which can take decisions for them. Each Church retains the constitutional right to ratify or to reject utterances or actions of the Council. The "authority" of the Council consists only "in the weight it carries with the Churches by its own wisdom" (William Temple).

4   2) *The purpose of the World Council of Churches is not to negotiate unions between Churches, which can only be done by the Churches themselves acting on their own initiative, but to bring the Churches into living contact with each other and to promote the study and discussion of the issues of Church unity.*

By its very existence and its activities the Council bears witness to the necessity of a clear manifestation of the oneness of the Church of Christ. But it remains the right and duty of each Church to draw from its ecumenical experi-

169

ence such consequences as it feels bound to do on the basis of its own convictions. No Church, therefore, need fear that the Council will press it into decisions concerning union with other Churches.

5   3) *The World Council cannot and should not be based on any one particular conception of the Church. It does not prejudge the ecclesiological problem.*

It is often suggested that the dominating or underlying conception of the Council is that of such and such a Church or such and such a school of theology. It may well be that at a certain particular conference or in a particular utterance one can find traces of the strong influence of a certain tradition or theology.

The Council as such cannot possibly become the instrument of one confession or school without losing its very *raison d'être*. There are room and space in the World Council for the ecclesiology of every Church which is ready to participate in the ecumenical conversation and which takes its stand on the Basis of the Council, which is "a fellowship of Churches which accept our Lord Jesus Christ as God and Saviour."

The World Council exists in order that different Churches may face their differences, and therefore no Church is obliged to change its ecclesiology as a consequence of membership in the World Council.

6   4) *Membership in the World Council of Churches does not imply that a Church treats its own conception of the Church as merely relative.*

There are critics, and not infrequently friends, of the ecumenical movement who criticize or praise it for its alleged inherent latitudinarianism. According to them the ecumenical movement stands for the fundamental equality of all Christian doctrines and conceptions of the Church and is, therefore, not concerned with the question of truth. This misunderstanding is due to the fact that ecumenism has in the minds of these persons become identified with certain particular theories about unity, which have indeed played a role in ecumenical history, but which do not represent the common view of the movement as a whole, and have never been officially endorsed by the World Council.

170

7   5) *Membership in the World Council does not imply the acceptance of a specific doctrine concerning the nature of Church unity.*

The Council stands for Church unity. But in its midst there are those who conceive unity wholly or largely as a full consensus in the realm of doctrine, others who conceive of it primarily as sacramental communion based on common church order, others who consider both indispensable, others who would only require unity in certain fundamentals of faith and order, again others who conceive the one Church exclusively as a universal spiritual fellowship, or hold that visible unity is inessential or even undesirable. But none of these conceptions can be called the ecumenical theory. The whole point of the ecumenical conversation is precisely that all these conceptions enter into dynamic relations with each other.

In particular, membership in the World Council does not imply acceptance or rejection of the doctrine that the unity of the Church consists in the unity of the invisible Church. Thus the statement in the Encyclical *Mystici Corporis* concerning what it considers the error of a spiritualized conception of unity does not apply to the World Council. The World Council does not "imagine a Church which one cannot see or touch, which would be only spiritual, in which numerous Christian bodies, though divided in matters of faith, would nevertheless be united through an invisible link." It does, however, include Churches which believe that the Church is essentially invisible as well as those which hold that visible unity is essential.

IV. THE ASSUMPTIONS UNDERLYING THE WORLD COUNCIL OF CHURCHES

8   We must now try to define the positive assumptions which underlie the World Council of Churches and the ecclesiological implications of membership in it.

1) *The member Churches of the Council believe that conversation, cooperation, and common witness of the Churches must be based on the common recognition that Christ is the Divine Head of the Body.*

The Basis of the World Council is the acknowledgment of the central fact that "other foundation can no man lay

171

than that is laid, even Jesus Christ." It is the expression of the conviction that the Lord of the Church is God-among-us Who continues to gather His children and to build His Church Himself.

Therefore, no relationship between the Churches can have any substance or promise unless it starts with the common submission of the Churches to the Headship of Jesus Christ in His Church. From different points of view Churches ask, "How can men with opposite convictions belong to one and the same federation of the faithful?" A clear answer to that question was given by the Orthodox delegates in Edinburgh 1937 when they said: "In spite of all our differences, our common Master and Lord is *one*— Jesus Christ who will lead us to a more and more close collaboration for the edifying of the Body of Christ."[2] The fact of Christ's Headship over His people compels all those who acknowledge Him to enter into real and close relationships with each other—even though they differ in many important points.

9   2) *The member Churches of the World Council believe on the basis of the New Testament that the Church of Christ is one.*

The ecumenical movement owes its existence to the fact that this article of the faith has again come home to men and women in many Churches with an inescapable force. As they face the discrepancy between the truth that there is and can be only one Church of Christ, and the fact that there exist so many Churches which claim to be Churches of Christ but are not in living unity with each other, they feel a holy dissatisfaction with the present situation. The Churches realize that it is a matter of simple Christian duty for each Church to do its utmost for the manifestation of the Church in its oneness, and to work and pray that Christ's purpose for His Church should be fulfilled.

10   3) *The member Churches recognize that the membership of the Church of Christ is more inclusive than the membership of their own Church body. They seek, therefore, to enter into living contact with those outside their own ranks who confess the Lordship of Christ.*

[2]From the statement presented to the Conference by Archbishop Germanos on behalf of the Orthodox delegates. The statement is not part of the conference report. It is printed in the minutes. Cf. Official Report. ed. by L. Hodgson, p. 157.

All the Christian Churches, including the Church of Rome, hold that there is no complete identity between the membership of the Church Universal and the membership of their own Church. They recognize that there are Church members *extra muros*, that these belong *aliquo modo* to the Church, or even that there is an *ecclesia extra ecclesiam*. This recognition finds expression in the fact that with very few exceptions the Christian Churches accept the baptism administered by other Churches as valid.

But the question arises what consequences are to be drawn from this teaching. Most often in Church history the Churches have only drawn the negative consequence that they should have no dealings with those outside their membership. The underlying assumption of the ecumenical movement is that each Church has a positive task to fulfil in this realm. That task is to seek fellowship with all those who, while not members of the same visible body, belong together as members of the mystical body. And the ecumenical movement is the place where this search and discovery take place.

11 4) *The member Churches of the World Council consider the relationship of other Churches to the Holy Catholic Church which the Creeds profess as a subject for mutual consideration. Nevertheless, membership does not imply that each Church must regard the other member Churches as Churches in the true and full sense of the word.*

There is a place in the World Council both for those Churches which recognize other Churches as Churches in the full and true sense, and for those who do not. But these divided Churches, even if they cannot yet accept each other as true and pure Churches, believe that they should not remain in isolation from each other, and consequently they have associated themselves in the World Council of Churches.

They know that differences of faith and order exist, but they recognize one another as serving the One Lord, and they wish to explore their differences in mutual respect, trusting that they may thus be led by the Holy Spirit to manifest their unity in Christ.

12   5) *The member Churches of the World Council recognize
in other Churches elements of the true Church. They
consider that this mutual recognition obliges them to
enter into a serious conversation with each other in the
hope that these elements of truth will lead to the
recognition of the full truth and to unity based on the
full truth.*

It is generally taught in the different Churches that other
Churches have certain elements of the true Church, in some
traditions called *vestigia ecclesiae.* Such elements are the
preaching of the Word, the teaching of the Holy Scriptures,
and the administration of the sacraments. These elements are more than pale shadows of the life of the true
Church. They are a fact of real promise and provide an
opportunity to strive by frank and brotherly intercourse
for the realization of a fuller unity. Moreover, Christians
of all ecclesiological views throughout the world, by the
preaching of the Gospel, brought men and women to
salvation by Christ, to newness of life in Him, and into
Christian fellowship with one another.

The ecumenical movement is based upon the conviction
that these "traces" are to be followed. The Churches should
not despise them as mere elements of truth but rejoice in
them as hopeful signs pointing toward real unity. For what
are these elements? Not dead remnants of the past but
powerful means by which God works. Questions may and
must be raised about the validity and purity of teaching
and sacramental life, but there can be no question that such
dynamic elements of Church life justify the hope that the
Churches which maintain them will be led into fuller truth.
It is through the ecumenical conversation that this recognition of truth is facilitated.

13   6) *The member Churches of the Council are willing to
consult together in seeking to learn of the Lord Jesus
Christ what witness He would have them to bear to
the world in His Name.*

Since the very *raison d'être* of the Church is to witness
to Christ, Churches cannot meet together without seeking
from their common Lord a common witness before the
world. This will not always be possible. But when it proves
possible thus to speak or act together, the Churches can

174

gratefully accept it as God's gracious gift that in spite of their disunity He has enabled them to render one and the same witness and that they may thus manifest something of the unity, the purpose of which is precisely "that the world may believe," and that they may "testify that the Father has sent the Son to be the Saviour of the world."

14 7) *A further practical implication of common membership in the World Council is that the member Churches should recognize their solidarity with each other, render assistance to each other in case of need, and refrain from such actions as are incompatible with brotherly relationships.*

Within the Council the Churches seek to deal with each other with a brotherly concern. This does not exclude extremely frank speaking to each other, in which within the Council the Churches ask each other searching questions and face their differences. But this is to be done for the building up the Body of Christ. This excludes a purely negative attitude of one Church to another. The positive affirmation of each Church's faith is to be welcomed, but actions incompatible with brotherly relationships towards other member Churches defeat the very purpose for which the Council has been created. On the contrary, these Churches should help each other in removing all obstacles to the free exercise of the Church's normal functions. And whenever a Church is in need or under persecution, it should be able to count on the help of the other Churches through the Council.

15 8) *The member Churches enter into spiritual relationships through which they seek to learn from each other and to give help to each other in order that the Body of Christ may be built up and that the life of the Churches may be renewed.*

It is the common teaching of the Churches that the Church as the temple of God is at the same time a building which has been built and a building which is being built. The Church has, therefore, aspects which belong to its very structure and essence and cannot be changed. But it has other aspects, which are subject to change. Thus the life of the Church, as it expresses itself in its witness to its own members and to the world, needs constant renewal.

The Churches can and should help each other in this realm by a mutual exchange of thought and of experience. This is the significance of the study-work of the World Council and of many other of its activities. There is no intention to impose any particular pattern of thought or life upon the Churches. But whatever insight has been received by one or more Churches is to be made available to all the Churches for the sake of the "building up of the Body of Christ."

16   None of these positive assumptions, implied in the existence of the World Council, is in conflict with the teachings of the member Churches.We believe therefore that no Church need fear that by entering into the World Council it is in danger of denying its heritage.

17   As the conversation between the Churches develops and as the Churches enter into closer contact with each other, they will no doubt have to face new decisions and problems. For the Council exists to break the deadlock between the Churches. But in no case can or will any Church be pressed to take a decision against its own conviction or desire. The Churches remain wholly free in the action which, on the basis of their convictions and in the light of their ecumenical contacts, they will or will not take.

18   A very real unity has been discovered in ecumenical meetings which is, to all who collaborate in the World Council, the most precious element of its life. It exists and we receive it again and again as an unmerited gift from the Lord. We praise God for this foretaste of the unity of His People and continue hopefully with the work to which He has called us together. For the Council exists to serve the Churches as they prepare to meet their Lord Who knows only one flock.

2.

THE CALLING
OF THE CHURCH
TO MISSION AND TO UNITY

*Received by the Central Committee at Rolle 1951 and
commended for study and comment in the Churches.*

1   I. THE PURPOSE OF THIS ENQUIRY

1. The problem of the relation of "Church" and "Mission"
has been before the minds of Christians for many decades.
The older Churches have only slowly and painfully learned
to accept the missionary obligation. The younger Churches
are slowly and painfully emerging from the period of
tutelage under foreign missions into independence as
Churches. The words "Church" and "Mission" still denote
in the minds of most Christians two different kinds of institution. Yet we know that these two things cannot rightly
be separated. . . .

(2-4)

5   II. TERMINOLOGY

It is necessary to point out that thinking on these issues
is often confused by lack of clarity in the use of terms. It
is extremely difficult to achieve uniformity because, quite
apart from problems of translation, even the same English
word carries very different overtones of meaning in different
areas. The words "mission" and "community" are examples
which have occurred during our discussion. We would espe-

cially draw attention to the recent confusion in the use of the word "ecumenical." It is important to insist that this word, which comes from the Greek word for the whole inhabited earth, is properly used to describe everything that relates to the whole task of the whole Church to bring the Gospel to the whole world. It therefore covers equally the missionary movement and the movement toward unity, and must not be used to describe the latter in contradistinction to the former. We believe that a real service will be rendered to true thinking on these subjects in the Churches if we so use this word that it covers both Unity and Mission in the context of the whole world. . . .

6   Our concern in this study is the recovery in thought, in action, and in organization, of the true unity between the Church's mission to the world (its Apostolate) and the Church's obligation to be one.

III. THE BIBLICAL BASIS FOR THE CHURCH'S UNITY AND APOSTOLICITY

7   The division in our thought and practice between "Church" and "Mission" can be overcome only as we return to Christ Himself, in Whom the Church has its being and its task, and to a fresh understanding of what He has done, is doing, and will do. God's eternal purpose is to "sum up all things in Christ." According to this purpose He has reconciled us to Himself and to one another through the Cross and has built us together to be a habitation of God in the Spirit. In reconciling us to Himself in Christ He has at the same time made us His ambassadors beseeching others to be reconciled to Him. He has made us members in the Body of Christ, and that means that we are both members one of another and also committed thereby to partnership in His redeeming mission.

8   In more detail we may say that the Church's unity and apostolicity rests upon the whole redeeming work of Christ—past, present, and future.

    (a) It rests upon His finished work upon the Cross. He has wrought the atonement between man and God —an atonement for the whole human race. As we receive the reconciliation, we are both reconciled to one another, and also constrained by His love to bring to all men the good news of reconciliation.

(b) It rests upon His continuing work as the risen Lord Who, having conquered sin and death, sits at God's right hand, and by His spirit communicates to us His own fulness. By His spirit we are joined as members in His body, committed to His redemptive mission. We are enabled to abide in Him, and so to bear fruit. We are given power to be His witnesses to all the nations and to gather together peoples of all races and tongues.

(c) It rests upon His promise that He will come again. In His final victory the Kingdoms of the world will be His, there will be one flock as there is one Shepherd, and all things will be summed up in Him. But first the Gospel of the Kingdom is to be preached throughout the whole world. In His mercy he gives us time and strength to fulfil this task.

9   Thus the obligation to take the Gospel to the whole world, and the obligation to draw all Christ's people together both rest upon Christ's whole work, and are indissolubly connected. Every attempt to separate these two tasks violates the wholeness of Christ's ministry to the world. Both of them are, in the strict sense of the word, essential to the being of the Church and fulfilment of its function as the Body of Christ.

10   *Note:* There are two important matters in which we are not agreed as to the interpretation of the biblical revelation, and on these we consider that study is needed.

(a) While we are agreed that unity is of the essence of the Church, we are not agreed as to the visible forms in which this unity is to be expressed.

(b) While we are agreed in looking for Christ's final victory, we are not agreed as to the manner of his victory, and as to its relation to what we may rightly hope for within history.

IV. IMPLICATONS FOR THE LIFE OF THE CHURCH

11   1. We recognize with thankfulness all the signs of the Church's acknowledgment of its missionary nature—the witness of many congregations and groups, the great work of "home and foreign" missions, and the faithful witness of countless individuals.

179

12   2. Yet we have to confess with deep penitence that the normal life of our Churches does *not* express the truth that to be a Christian is necessarily to be involved in a mission to the whole world.

(a) The average congregation is apt to be an introverted community which does not think primarily of its obligation to bring the knowledge of Christ to its whole neighbourhood and to the whole world, and this introversion is apt to mark the life, thought, and leadership of the whole Church. This applies to the younger Churches as well as to the older.

(b) Even where the obligation is acknowledged and acted upon, such action tends to take the form of a separate "mission" supported by the congregation but not regarded as the responsibility of every member.

(c) Normal theological study and teaching does not sufficiently concern itself with the task of bringing the Gospel to those outside. It largely presupposes a static rather than a missionary Church.

(d) The great world missionary enterprise of the Churches has naturally created its own instruments and organizations, and these tend to be somewhat separate from the rest of the life of the Churches. It is too easy to be a church member without feeling oneself committed to the world-wide missionary task.

13   3. We are thankful to know of many bold attempts to break through this situation and to develop new patterns of church life which shall demonstrate the essentially dynamic and missionary character of the Church. . . .

14   4. As we see how many Churches in our own day are being stripped of many things which have been regarded as necessary—such as buildings, funds, institutions, and privileged posiitons—we are led to believe that God is in this way forcing His Church to come out into the open and to commit itself afresh in a dynamic encounter with the world. We pray that the Church everywhere may learn to abandon all trust in earthly securities and to face the world with that courage which is now the very condition of existence for some of our member Churches.

V. IMPLICATIONS FOR THE WORLD MISSIONARY TASK

15   1. The great missionary movement of the recent centuries has under God brought into being a Church which is in some sense world-wide. We confess with gratitude that this is a mighty work of God's Spirit working through His Church even when the Church's obedience was in many ways deeply imperfect. Despite all its limitations and imperfections this movement has been the greatest spiritual movement of its kind in history. It is a movement moreover which, even at the present time, engages the devotion and represents the sacrificial giving of a great multitude of Christian people.

16   2. We have nevertheless to acknowledge with penitence that this great movement has in many respects been marred by the defects of the Churches from which the mission went forth. In particular:

(a) There has been an unconscious confusion of the unchanging Gospel with the particular cultural, economic, and institutional forms of the older Churches.

(b) The result has been that missionaries of the older Churches have often been instrumental in bringing into being Churches which are too largely replicas of those from which they had come. We have therefore to admit that there has been an element of cultural domination in the work of missions, and that those engaged in the missionary enterprise have often relied too much upon their own precept, example, and influence and have not given sufficient freedom to the younger Churches to express their Christian obedience in new forms under the guidance of the Holy Spirit.

(c) This has inevitably resulted in the creation of Churches which, even though technically independent, are yet compelled to depend upon the older Churches for support in leadership and finance because they are too foreign in form.

(d) Moreover, because of the divisions in the older Churches, the various missions of many denominations from many lands have created confusion and division of the Christian witness among non-Christian peoples.

(e) We have to admit that too large a proportion of the great volume of missionary giving and service which flows out from the older Churches is at present required to prop up relatively static younger Churches, rather than to make new advances for the Gospel.

17   3. We are therefore led to urge that the time is ripe for a fresh study of missionary principles and practice, and especially for a very earnest reconsideration of our present methods in the light of the Bible. . . . Our aim must be a partnership between older and younger Churches in which the strength of the former is not exhausted in the support of the latter, but in which older and younger Churches together can devote their combined strength to the vast unfinished mission of the Church to all men and all nations. . . .

18-20

3.

CHRISTIAN WITNESS, PROSELYTISM, AND RELIGIOUS LIBERTY

Adopted by the Central Commitee
at St. Andrews 1960 for transmission
to the member Churches for
consideration and comment

1   The Central Committee decided at its meeting in Evanston (1954) that, in view of difficulties which had arisen affecting relationships between member churches of the World Council of Churches, a Commission should be appointed for the further study of "Proselytism and Religious Liberty."

2   This Commission, meeting at Arnoldshain, Germany, in July, 1956, prepared a provisional report under the revised title "Christian Witness, Proselytism, and Religious Liberty in the Setting of the World Council of Churches." This change in title reflects the recognition that proselytism in its derogatory meaning represents a corruption of Christian witness or evangelism. It also underscores the fact that it is primarily as a problem affecting the relationships of member churches of the World Council of Churches that the study was authorized.

3   The provisional report of the Commission was amended by a committee of the Central Committee at Galyatetö,

183

Hungary, in August, 1956, and approved by the Central Committee for submission to the member churches to set forward our common self-examination on this difficult problem in our relationships with one another and with other churches. The provisional report was published in the *Ecumenical Review* of October, 1956.

4   When the question of taking further action with regard to the provisional report was raised at the meeting of the Central Committee at Rhodes in 1959 and considered by a Reference Committee, it was felt that the churches had not given sufficient response to guide the Central Committee. It therefore authorized that the provisional report be transmitted again to the member churches requesting replies by March 1, 1960. It also asked the Commission to consider the advice of the churches and the comments of the Reference Committee and to prepare a statement of policy for submission to the Central Committee in 1960 "for consideration, adoption, and recommendation to the Third Assembly, in the hope that such a policy statement would prove acceptable and helpful to the churches in their relationship with one another.

5   In the meantime, the discussion of the proposed integration of the World Council of Churches and the International Missionary Council had contributed added interest to the study.

6   This revised report, drafted by the Commission at St. Andrews in August, 1960, in the light of a substantial volume of careful responses from a variety of member churches and after further study, is submitted to the Central Committee in accordance with its request.

7   As our study has proceeded, it has become increasingly clear that the poles of our problem are to be found in the right and duty of free Christian witness on the one hand, and in the obligation of an ecumenical fellowship to manifest the visible unity of the Church as the Body of Christ on the other hand. The tension is between the two, and our problem is to deal justly with both in truth and love.

8   Behind the tension lies the whole ecclesiological problem, which is a major concern in our continuous ecumenical association. The territorial principle is an aspect of that problem. Unsolved problems of faith and order also contribute to the tension.

9   Consequently, this is a modest and limited report. It attempts not so much to resolve the basic issues as to clarify the nature of the tension and to suggest some guiding principles with regard to the spirit and nature of the relationships within which the churches may best deal with the issues. Specific rules cannot be prescribed for all national and local situations. Churches which live together are therefore encouraged to strive to achieve mutual understanding, earnestly taking into consideration the ecumenical perspective of this report.

10   While this report is primarily concerned with relations between the member churches of the World Council, we are not unmindful of its implication for our relationships with other churches and religious groups. Our covenant as "churches which accept our Lord Jesus Christ as God and Saviour" to "stay together" in brotherly counsel and mutual aid calls for special self-searching in the way we exercise our freedom of witness. But any light we gain as to our right relations with one another is surely relevant to our relations with other churches.

11   I. THE USE OF THE TERMS: CHRISTIAN WITNESS, RELIGIOUS LIBERTY, AND PROSELYTISM

     Various meanings have been attached to the terms "witness," "religious liberty," "proselytism." The sense in which we use them in the present discussion needs to be made clear. This is especially true of "proselytism," which today has an almost completely derogatory sense: probably no church and no missionary society involved in the ecumenical movement would wish to call itself a "proselytizing body." It does not seem possible, in practice, to restore the good connotation which the word "proselyte" once carried. Thus "proselytizing" has come to be set over against true obedience to the Great Commission: "Go therefore and make disciples of all nations, baptizing them in the name of the Father and of the Son and of the Holy Spirit, teaching them to observe all that I have commanded you...." (Matthew 28:19-20).

12   For this true obedience the words evangelism, apostolate, soul-winning, witness, and others are now in common use. In this report the word "witness" will be employed.

a) *Christian Witness*

185

13   Witness in word and deed is the essential mission and responsibility of every Christian and of every church. All disciples stand under the Great Commission of the one Lord.

14   The purpose of witness is to persuade persons to accept the supreme authority of Christ, to commit themselves to Him, and to render Him loving service in the fellowship of His Church. The witness of Christians to Jesus Christ requires both personal and corporate testimony to the truth as it has been revealed to them, but no human testimony to the truth as it is in Jesus Christ can reflect that truth in its fullness. Even when inwardly compelled to testify against that which appears erroneous in some other religious belief or practice, he who would bear a true witness cannot but be humble and honest. He knows but one weight and one measure, the same for himself as for others.

15   Such an act of witness seeks a response which contributes to the upbuilding of the fellowship of those who acknowledge the Lordship of Christ. A person enters that fellowship by becoming a member of one of the several existing ecclesiastical communities. Both witness and response must therefore, of present necessity, take place within the existing situation of division in the Church.

16   This situation gives rise to problems in the relationships between the churches when one church yields to the temptation to seek its own institutional advantage at the cost of real or seeming disadvantage to another. It is a purpose of the World Council of Churches to help the several churches so to carry on their witness as to strengthen one another, and thus by their combined effort in mutual cooperation to spread the Gospel more effectively.

b) *Religious Liberty*

17   God's truth and love are given in freedom and call for a free response.

18   God does not coerce men to respond to His love; and the revelation of God in Christ is a revelation that men are not forced to accept. He calls men to make a willing and obedient response to Him in faith, to answer with a free and confident "yes" to the eternal action of His love in which He reveals Himself. This utterly free assent is undermined and destroyed when human coercion enters in. Human coercion denies the respect for every individual person which God's loving action in Christ affirms. The

non-coercive method and spirit of Christ is in itself the condemnation of all attempts to force man's religious beliefs or to purchase their allegiance, and for the Christian it is the ground of religious liberty.

19   Every Christian has the liberty individually or in the corporate body of a church or other group to put his whole existence under the authority of God, to believe, pray, worship, and proclaim Christ, as well as to live in accordance with His will, in the church of his choice according to his own conscience. For such witness and service churches and individuals should have equality before the law.

20   It also follows that the conscience of persons whose religious faith and convictions differ from our own must be recognized and respected.

21   The right of all men to freedom of conscience and freedom of religious belief and practice is recognized by law in most countries. The article on religious liberty in the Universal Declaration of Human Rights is consistent with Christian conviction in this matter: "Everyone has the right to freedom of thought, conscience, and religion. This right includes the freedom to change his religion or belief, and freedom, either alone or in community with others, and in public or in private, to manifest his religion or belief, in teaching, practice, worship, and observance."

22   Liberty is not absolute, for it must not be exercised in such a way as to impair the Golden Rule (Matt. 7:12).

c) *Proselytism*

23   Proselytism is not something absolutely different from witness: it is the corruption of witness. Witness is corrupted when cajolery, bribery, undue pressure, or intimidation are used—subtly or openly—to bring about seeming conversion; when we put the success of our church before the honour of Christ; when we commit the dishonesty of comparing the ideal of our own church with the actual achievement of another; when we seek to advance our own cause by bearing false witness against another church; when personal or corporate self-seeking replaces love for every individual soul with whom we are concerned. Such corruption of the Christian witness indicates lack of confidence in the power of the Holy Spirit, lack of respect for the nature of man, and lack of recognition of the true character of the Gospel. It is very easy to recognize these

faults and sins in others; it is necessary to acknowledge that we are all liable to fall into one or the other of them ourselves.

24 Since the difference between witness and proselytism is a matter of purpose, motive, and spirit, as well as of means, objective criteria alone cannot adequately distinguish between the two. Nevertheless such criteria do exist, and some general objective standards of practice are possible. The fourth section of this report attempts to describe such standards in the hope that a larger measure of mutual understanding can thereby be attained among the churches, thus rendering their common witness for Christ more faithful and more convincing.

II. BACKGROUND

25 The issues with which this study is concerned have existed within the ecumenical movement from its very beginning. In 1920 the well-known Encyclical of the Ecumenical Patriarchate with its strong plea for cooperation among the churches asked for a definite cessation of proselytizing activities. When in the same year in Geneva the preliminary meeting of "Faith and Order" and of "Life and Work" took place, the issue was again brought up by the Orthodox representatives. In the larger and smaller ecumenical conferences during the next decades the question was often raised, but no definite action was taken. At the time when the ecclesiological significance of the World Council of Churches was discussed this particular aspect of inter-church relationships was touched upon only very briefly. The Toronto statement says that churches should "refrain from such actions as are incompatible with brotherly relationships" and develops this point in the following manner: "The positive affirmation of each church's faith is to be welcomed, but actions incompatible with brotherly relationships toward other member churches defeat the very purpose for which the Council has been created."[1] It was, however, not said just what is implied in this constructive relationship.

26 This extremely brief reference to the history of the discussion shows that these issues call for honest and careful consideration by the member churches. Failure to deal

[1]See To 14.

with them seriously would leave unnecessary misunderstanding in the relationships between member churches in certain areas.

27   Behind the issues of "proselytism" and of religious liberty here considered, there lie various historical causes, among which are the following:

1. In the modern age, technological and sociological developments in all parts of our world are changing radically the previously established patterns of human communities. Because means of communication and of mobility have greatly increased, religious and cultural communities no longer find it possible to remain closed to outside influences, but are increasingly being influenced by ideas and movements from outside. It is only necessary to mention the far-reaching influence of newsprint and literature, radio and films, as well as the presence of foreigners and of foreign influences of all types in most countries. National boundary lines cannot any longer isolate a culture. These pervasive and dynamic influences are such that they could only be thwarted by forcible repression—as by cutting off circulation of newsprint and literature, by jamming radio communication, by forbidding free travel and entry into a country.

28   2. In recent years, religious and cultural communities find themselves extended far beyond their original national and ethnic borders. Refugee resettlement as well as other forms of migration have led to the extension of Orthodox, Protestant, and Roman Catholic communities into new territories.

29   3. In the area of religious and church relationships the most disturbing situations are found where a particular church has been historically identified with the total life and culture of a country or territory, whether or not as a legally established or "state church," and is confronted by religious movements stemming from outside or appearing as spontaneous movements of renewal threatening its unity from within the territory.

30   The anxiety and resistance manifested by the church hitherto in sole or dominant occupancy of a territory cannot fairly be ascribed simply to a desire to maintain a privileged monopoly. These may also express a rightful concern for the preservation of the unity and integrity of the church of the nation, and for fidelity to the principle that the church of the territory has a responsibility for the whole

human community in which it is set. Indeed we are witnessing, especially in Asia and Africa, vigorous efforts to achieve regional or national church unity. These concerns are often re-enforced by nationalist sentiment and the serious desire to preserve the cultural unity of a people.

31 While it is of the utmost importance that we understand sympathetically these concerns and the real values involved, it is equally important that we recognize the problems they present to religious liberty, and the fact that in other parts of the world churches have found new freedom and vitality in more open and diversified societies.

32 4. In the 19th century tensions arose out of new contacts between Christians of different churches in areas taken as fields of foreign missionary activity. In some cases, missions directed towards non-Christians found themselves working among and drawing to themselves members of other Christian churches already long established in these lands. In other cases, missions were directed towards those who were believed to be lapsed or imperfectly evangelized members of other churches. At various periods "free churches" have sprung up or been planted in areas previously the exclusive province of "national churches" or "state churches." In recent years there has been a great increase in the number and activity of religious groups appealing for individual conversions, but sometimes with very little church-consciousness and with little or no interest in cooperation with others.

33 5. Interacting with these developments and situations is the fact that churches have become increasingly aware in recent centuries that Christian freedom is at the base of all liberties. Political and social philosophies of the 17th century and after have likewise placed a strong emphasis on liberty in all its forms, including religious liberty.

34 Churches all over the world find themselves confronted with the necessity of carrying out their mission in a new situation. Many churches in many areas are troubled by some form of "proselytism."

35 At the same time emergence of an organized ecumenical movement has given both a new focal point to the struggle for religious liberty and a new impetus to the claims of unity and fellowship. Our membership together in the World Council of Churches brings us a compelling incen-

tive and an effective instrument for the working out of our
new relationships to each other.

III. BASIC CONSIDERATIONS

36   1. Every Christian church is not only permitted but required freely and openly to bear its witness in the world,
seeking to bring persons into fellowship with God as revealed in Jesus Christ. Witnessing is a part of the church's
ministry of love, of its service to mankind.

37   2. The commandment to bear witness to the truth of
Christ and to seek to win others to that truth is valid in
relation not only to non-Christians but also to others who
have no living relationship to any Christian church..
Churches ought to rejoice whenever fresh influences quick-
en the faith of those committed to their pastoral care, even
if those influences come from outside their own structure.
Such a quickening witness, brought into the life of a given
church, should be concerned for the unity as well as for
the renewal of that church's life.

38   3. Should errors or abuses within a church result in
the distorting or obscuring of the central truths of the
Gospel and thereby jeopardize men's salvation, other
churches may feel bound to come to the rescue with a
faithful witness to the truth thus lost to view. Their
liberty to do so must be maintained. But before they undertake to establish another church, they must humbly ask
themselves whether there are not still to be found in the
existing church such signs of the presence of the Holy
Spirit that frank fraternal contact and cooperation with it
must be sought.

39   4. The Toronto Statement of the Central Committee of
the World Council of Churches sets forth some of our
present understandings of the ways in which member
churches regard one another:

  a) No Church by virtue of its membership in the World
     Council (e.g. Toronto, III. 3, 4, and 5) is under an
     obligation to suppress, truncate, or alter its full con-
     fession of truth, by which it stands or falls in its being
     and ministry as a church, for in so doing it would
     mutilate itself. It is not in the interest of the World
     Council to have mutilated churches as members. On
     the contrary, it aims to be a Council of whole, real,
     and genuine churches. This means that every member

191

church must be able to bring its full untruncated witness of the truth openly and joyfully into the Council and there give it full expression, without holding anything back.

b) Membership in the World Council does not imply that each church must regard the other member churches as churches in the true and full sense of the Word (IV. 4). This means that a church which in the light of its own confession must regard certain teachings of another member church as errors and heresies and certain of its practices as abuses cannot be compelled to withdraw or hold back its views because of the churches' common membership in the World Council, but can and indeed should continue in the future to hold and express its views in their full scope. The more frankly a church states its views in the Council or within the ecumenical fellowship, the less will be the need to state them in a round-about and undesirable way.

c) It is precisely within the ecumenical fellowship that this exchange should proceed to the fullest extent and without minimizing the difficulty and seriousness of the issues (IV. 7 and 8). It can be observed that churches will be most inclined toward proselytism, or, on the other hand, toward making charges of proselytism, when the psychological and spiritual atmosphere is such that churches either shrink from or are prevented from openly confessing the truth in their relations with each other.

d) Membership in the World Council places a moral obligation upon the churches to observe a particular attitude in this discussion. It would be inconsistent with this membership for one member church altogether to deny another member church the status of a church, or to regard it as entirely heretical or hopelessly given over to abuses, so that its members could only be helped by being rescued from it. On the basis of their common confession of Jesus Christ as God and Saviour and as the One Head of the Church, member churches jointly recognize "hopeful signs" in each other (IV. 1 and 5).

192

40   5. Witnessing within the ecumenical fellowship takes place in various ways and the following may be mentioned as examples:

   a) Unofficial discussion and personal encounter between individuals in search of truth.

   b) Official discussion between one church and another, each giving full weight to its own confession.

   c) An important approach within the framework of the World Council is seen in the work of Inter-Church Aid, when one church helps another church to recover a healthier life of its own; one church, with the agreement of another, helps it to carry out work of evangelistic, catechetical, or educational character or renders some other service on behalf of members of that other church with the aim not only of leaving them in their own church, but helping them to be more faithful to it and to become better Christians there. It is clear that this approach demands a great degree of selflessness and humility on the part of both churches.

IV. RECOMMENDATIONS FOR CONTINUING CONSIDERATION BY THE MEMBER CHURCHES

41   During the past years several issues treated in this report have received the consideration of many of the member churches. The Central Committee of the World Council of Churches has given attention to them at several of its meetings. It is widely recognized that these issues must remain a continuing concern of churches drawn together, and resolved to stay together, in ecumenical fellowship as member churches of the World Council. It has been our purpose to contribute to a clarification and a deeper understanding of the issues and problems that confront us together.

42   At the same time it must be recognized that the actual situation which churches in different parts of the world face in their relationships to one another are extremely diverse. Where there are problems in these relationships, they can generally best be dealt with by the churches themselves within a particular geographical area—local, national, or regional—as they confront one another.

43   Where there are problems in the relationships of churches to one another, we believe that solutions will be found not so much by rules and regulations as by right attitudes and reconciling actions.

44   Moreover, even if rules and regulations were desirable, the World Council of Churches by its nature and according to its Constitution has neither the authority nor the intent to exercise control over the member churches or to legislate for them, and is indeed explicitly prevented by its Constitution from doing so. It is even more obvious that the World Council cannot control churches or religious groups which have no relation to it. The influence of its statements derives from their intrinsic merit and from the fact that they express the convictions of responsible representatives of the churches.

45   Having due regard for the nature of the ecumenical fellowship represented by the World Council of Churches, we at the same time recognize certain principles which we believe should guide churches in their mutual relationships and which, if followed, might provide objective and generally applicable standards of practice.

46   The principles here set forth lay no claim to finality. We have found, however, that they are already receiving sympathetic consideration in many of the member churches. The following principles are set forth in the hope and belief that they may be helpful to the churches as they examine their own situation, and that they may provide churches and councils of churches with a useful basis for further study and consideration on a local, national, and regional basis of the issues treated in this report.

47   1. That we in our churches respect the convictions of other churches whose conception and practice of church membership differ from our own, and consider it our Christian duty to pray for one another and to help each other rise above our respective shortcomings through frank theological interchange, experiences of common worship, and concrete acts of mutual service; and that we recognize it as our obligation, when in exceptional cases private or public criticism of another church seems to be required of us, first to examine ourselves and always to speak the truth in love and to the edification of the churches.

48   2. That we recognize it as the primary duty of every awakened Christian to strive prayerfully for the renewal of that church in which he is a member;

49   3. That we recognize the right of the mature individual to change his church allegiance if he becomes convinced that such change of allegiance is God's will for him;

50   4. That since grave obstacles to brotherly relationships between churches are created when some churches are denied the religious liberty which is accorded to others, all Christians should work towards the establishing and maintenance of religious liberty for all churches and all their members in every land;

51   5. That we disavow any church action by which material or social advantages are offered to influence a person's church affliliation, or undue pressures are brought to bear on persons in times of helplessness or stress;

52   6. That while it is proper for churches to make clear their position with regard to marriages between persons belonging to different communions, the conscientious decision of marriage partners as to their future church allegiance should be respected;

53   7. That before a young child is received into the membership of a church other than that of the present affiliation of the parents or guardian, a due pastoral concern for the unity of the family should be exercised; and where the proposed change of affiliation is contrary to the desire of those directly responsible for the child's nurture and up-bringing, he (or she) should not be received into the membership of the other church unless there be reason of exceptional weight;

54   8. That due pastoral care should be exercised before receiving anyone into the membership of a church if he is already, as the member of another church, under discipline by that church, or if there is evidence that his reasons for seeking membership in a different church are worldly or unworthy;

55   9. That whenever a member of one church desires to be received into the membership of another church, direct consultation should be sought between the churches concerned; but if conscientious motives and sound reasons are apparent, no obstacle should be placed in the way of such change of membership before or after its accomplishment;

56   10. That while there may be situations where a church already present in a given area seems to be so inadequate in its witness to Christ as to call for more faithful witness and proclamation of the Gospel to its members, the first effort of other churches should be patiently to help that church towards its renewal and the strengthening of its own witness and ministry;

57   11. That we should aid churches in areas where they are at work, by offering fraternal workers and exchanges of personnel as well as by sharing knowledge and skills and resources, rather than by establishing a competing mission of some other church.

58   In our relationships in the World Council of Churches, the member churches are all called to show such restraint in their exercise of religious liberty as to avoid the causing of offence, and in the fullest possible measure to respect the convictions of other churches. We therefore call upon the member churches to disavow proselytism as defined in this report.

59   We believe that the member churches should be asked to give thoughtful and prayerful consideration to the matters with which this report is concerned, so that in their dealings with each other they may be mindful of the obligations inherent in the ecumenical fellowship.

III.

Various Documents
on the Faith
and Order Movement

1.

Joint Commission Appointed to Arrange for a World Conference on Faith and Order

Report on Plan and Scope (1911)[1]

I. THE ULTIMATE AIM AND PURPOSE

The work of the Conference is undertaken with the definite hope that it may help to prepare the way for the outward and visible reunion of all who confess our Lord Jesus Christ as God and Saviour, and for the fulfillment of our Lord's prayer, "That they all may be one."

II. THE IMMEDIATE PURPOSE AND THE SCOPE OF THE PRESENT UNDERTAKING

The purpose and the scope of this Commission are defined by the resolution of the General Convention and the report of the Committee recommending that resolution. The immediate purpose is to bring about as "the next step towards unity" a Conference for the consideration of questions of Faith and Order, to

[1]Cf. Faith and Order, numbered publications, Series 1, 3. In 1910 the General convention of the Protestant Episcopal church in the USA adopted the following resolution: . . . that a joint commission be appointed to bring about a Conference for the consideration of questions touching Faith and Order and that all Christian Communions throughout the world which confess our Lord Jesus Christ as God and Saviour be asked to unite with us in arranging for and conducting such a conference . . . This commission adopted in the following year the report Plan and Scope, extracts of which are given here.

be participated in by representatives of the whole Christian world, both Catholic and Protestant.

This work is to be undertaken in "the belief that the beginnings of unity are to be found in the clear statement and full consideration of those things in which we differ, as well as of those things in which we are at one."

It is ordered "that all Christian Communions throughout the world which confess our Lord Jesus Christ as God and Saviour be asked to unite with us in arranging for and conducting such a conference."

The action taken by the Convention contemplates "a Conference for the purpose of study and discussion without power to legislate or to adopt resolutions."

To reemphasize these important points:

1. The Conference is for the definite purpose of considering those things in which we differ, in the hope that a better understanding of divergent views of Faith and Order will result in a deepened desire for reunion and in official action on the part of the separated Communions themselves. It is the business of the Conference, not to take such official action, but to inspire it and to prepare the way for it.

2. All Christian Communions are to be asked "to unite with us in arranging for and conducting" the Conference. We, ourselves, are to take only preliminary action, and at the earliest moment possible are to act in association with others. Formal association for joint action can be effected only after a sufficient number of commissions shall have been appointed, and sufficient opportunity to appoint such commissions shall have been afforded to all Communions, both Catholic and Protestant.

3. The Conference will have no power to commit any participating Communion upon any point.

III. GENERAL PLAN OF ACTION

Obviously any plan outlined at present can be only tentative. To bring the idea of the Conference more definitely before our minds, it is suggested that, at the proper times, appropriate action be taken along the following lines:

1. That the prayers of all Christian people be asked for God's blessing upon this undertaking.

2. That as soon as practicable similar commissions or committees be appointed by Christian Communions throughout the

world, such commissions or committees be independent, though cooperating.

3. That arrangements be made for such joint meetings of such Commissions as may be found convenient.

4. That final plans and arrangements for the World Conference be worked out by an executive body constituted by the several action of such commissions.

2.

The Constitution
of The Commission
on Faith and Order[2]

TITLE

1. The Commission shall be called the Commission on Faith and Order of the World Council of Churches.

MEANINGS

2. In this Constitution:

The Commission means the above-named Commission on Faith and Order of the World Council of Churches.

The Working Committee means the Working Committee of the Commission on Faith and Order.

The Council means the above-named World Council of Churches

The Assembly means the Assembly of the World Council.

The Central Committee means the Central Committee of the World Council.

FUNCTIONS

3. The functions of the Commission are:

(i) To proclaim the essential oneness of the Church of Christ and to keep prominently before the World Council and the Churches the obligation to manifest that unity and its urgency for world mission and evangelism.

[2]As accepted at the Third World Conference on Faith and Order, Lund, 1952, and subsequently revised by the Second Assembly of the World Council of Churches, Evanston, 1954, by the Central Committee, Davos, 1955, and by the Commission on Faith and Order and the Central Committee, St. Andrews, 1960, and Paris, 1962.

(ii) To study questions of faith, order, and worship with the relevant social, cultural, political, racial, and other factors in their bearing on the unity of the Church.

(iii) To study the theological implications of the existence of the ecumenical movement.

(iv) To study matters in the present relationships of the Churches to one another which cause difficulties and need theological clarification.

(v) To provide information concerning actual steps taken by the Churches towards reunion.

4. All activities of the Commission shall be in accordance with the four principles of the Faith and Order Movement, viz.:

(i) Its main work is to draw Churches out of isolation into conference, in which none is to be asked to be disloyal to or to compromise its convictions, but to seek to explain them to others while seeking to understand their points of view. Irreconcilable differences are to be recorded as honestly as agreements. (ii) Its conferences are to be conferences of delegates officially appointed by the Churches to represent them. (iii) The invitation to take part in these conferences is addressed to Christian Churches throughout the world which accept our Lord Jesus Christ as God and Saviour. (iv) Only Churches themselves are competent to take actual steps towards reunion by entering into negotiations with one another. The work of the Movement is not to formulate schemes and tell the Churches what they ought to do, but to act as the handmaid of the Churches in the preparatory work of clearing away misunderstandings, discussing obstacles to reunion, and issuing reports which are submitted to the Churches for their consideration.

ORGANIZATION

5. (i) World Conferences on Faith and Order are to be held when main subjects are ready for submission to the Churches, and when, on recommendation of the Commission on Faith and Order, the Central Committee so decides.

(ii) The Commission on Faith and Order shall consist of 100 members appointed by the Assembly of the World Council, with power to nominate additional members up to the number of 20 for appointment by the Central Committee, all these to hold office until the next Assembly (subject, however, to any revision advised by a World Conference on Faith and Order as hereinafter provided). At each Assembly the list of membership shall be revised in the light of recommendations made by the Commission. When a World Conference is held, it shall advise the Central Committee on any necessary revision of the membership of the Commission between that Conference and the next Assembly. In making appointments care shall be taken to secure the adequate geographical and confessional representation of Churches.

The Commission may include members of Churches which accept our Lord Jesus Christ as God and Saviour but are not members of the World Council.

Vacancies shall be filled by the Central Committee on the recommendation of the Commission.

Before appointments are made, steps shall be taken to ensure that the appointments proposed are acceptable to the Churches concerned.

(iii) The Commission shall normally meet every three years but may be called together at any time when major theological commission reports need to be reviewed by a larger body than the Working Committee.

(iv) The Commission shall nominate from its own members, for appointment by the Central Committee, a Working Committee of not more than 22 members with power to nominate not more than 3 additional members. The Chairman of the Commission shall also be a member *ex officio* of the Working Committee. The Working Committee shall normally meet annually and shall be responsible (a) for administration (b) for directing the study work and other activities of Faith and Order and (c) for co-operation with other agencies of the World Council.

Vacancies in the Working Committee shall be filled by the Working Committee itself from the membership of the Commission and submitted to the Central Committee for appointment.

(v) There shall be various theological commissions set up by the Commission or Working Committee. Theological commissions may include as members or consultants persons who are not members of the Commission.

MEETINGS OF THE COMMISSION

6. The Chairman of the Commission, or in his absence one of the Vice-Chairmen, shall preside at meetings of the Commission. In the absence of these officers, the meeting shall elect its

own Chairman. One-sixth of the total membership shall constitute a quorum.

7. The notices of meetings shall be issued by the Secretary.

8. Members of the Commission can name substitutes to represent them at meetings at which they are unable to be present themselves.

9. On questions of Faith and Order the Commission shall not adopt any resolutions, but shall confine itself to recording for the information of the Churches such agreements and disagreements as are discovered.

10. Questions of procedure and the conduct of the business of the Commission shall be decided by a majority vote of those present and voting.

11. The Working Committee may, either at a meeting of the Commission or previously, determine the rules of procedure and of debate for the meeting.

12. Persons not being members of the Commission may be invited by the Chairman or the Secretary to be present and speak, but they cannot vote.

CHAIRMAN

13. The Chairman shall be elected by a majority of votes at a duly convened meeting of the Commission, on the nomination of the Working Committee.

14. The Chairman shall hold office for three years from the date of his appointment, but shall be eligible for re-election.

15. In the event of the office of Chairman falling vacant by reason of resignation, incapacity or death, the two Vice-Chairmen and the Chairman of the Working Committee shall be together responsible for the appointment of an acting Chairman until such time as a meeting of the Commission can be called.

VICE-CHAIRMEN

16. Two Vice-Chairmen shall be elected by the Commission on the nomination of the Working Committee, shall hold office for three years, and shall be eligible for re-election.

THE SECRETARIAT

17. There shall be at least one Secretary who shall be a member of the staff of the Council employed for the work of the Commission on a full-time basis.

18. The Secretary or Secretaries shall be nominated by the Commission to the Central Committee.

19. It shall be the special responsibility of the Secretary to maintain full consultation and co-operation with the General Secretariat and with the other Departments of the Council, and particularly with the Division of Studies.

20. The salaries or honoraria to be paid to the Secretary or Secretaries shall be determined by the Working Committee and the officers of the Council in consultation.

THE WORKING COMMITTEE

21. The Commission shall appoint the Chairman of the Working Committee.

22. Members of the Working Committee shall hold office until the next meeting of the Commission, when the list of membership shall be revised.

23. The Working Committee shall have power to act on behalf of the Commission in all matters where action is required before a meeting of the Commission can be convened.

24. The Working Committee shall meet at such times and places as the Chairman and the Secretary shall decide to be required for the performance of its duty.

25. The quorum for a meeting of the Working Committee shall be seven members present.

26. If at any time when it is inconvenient to convene a meeting the Chairman and Secretary shall decide that there is business needing an immediate decision by the Working Committee, it shall be permissible for them to obtain by post the opinions of its members and the majority opinion thus ascertained shall be treated as equivalent to the decision of a duly convened meeting.

THE DEPARTMENT

27. The Chairman, Vice-Chairmen, Secretaries, Chairman of the Working Committee, and the Chairmen of Theological Commissions shall together be known as the Council's Faith and Order Department.

28. The Department shall be responsible for continuously carrying on the work of the Commission between meetings of the Commission and the Working Committee, both by (i) promoting the studies of the Theological Commissions and (ii) following all developments in the matter of the union of Churches and keeping all the Churches informed of these developments.

It shall maintain full consultation and cooperation with the Division of Studies of the Council.

29. The Secretaries shall be the only officers of the Commission employed by the Council on a full-time basis; the other members of the Department shall be persons giving part-time service to the Commission whilst being also actively engaged in the service of their own Churches.

THE THEOLOGICAL COMMISSIONS

30. The work of the Theological Commissions shall be to prepare reports which may serve as the basis for discussion in the Commission, at the Assemblies of the World Council, or at Conferences on Faith and Order, on the Subjects referred to them under §5 (v) above.

31. Each Theological Commission shall be composed of a Chairman, Vice-Chairman, and Secretary with other members chosen for their special competence in the particular field of study and representing as wide a variety as possible of ecclesiastical traditions. The Chairman, Vice-Chairman, and Secretary shall be appointed by the Commision, and they then select and appoint the other members in consultation with the Working Committee, or in case of emergency with the Secretary of the Commission.

THE BUDGET

32. The Commission's financial year shall run from 1st January to 31st December.

33. An annual budget of expenditure shall be drawn up by the Secretary in consultation with the Finance Committee of the Council; it shall be submitted to the Working Committee for its approval and when so approved shall be submitted to the Council for final adoption. Copies shall then be sent to all members of the Commission.

34. The budget shall specify the amount allocated for the expenses of each Theological Commission, and each Theological Commission shall be responsible for deciding its manner of using its allocation within the limits prescribed in the budget.

REVISION

35. Any amendment to this Constitution shall be submitted by the Faith and Order Commission and must be approved by the Assembly or the Central Committee.

3.

Report of the Commission on Faith and Order to the Central Committee on the Subject of the Future of Faith and Order[3]

The Faith and Order movement was born in the hope that it would be, under God, a help to the churches in realizing His will for the unity of the Church. The formation of the World Council of Churches, and the incorporation of Faith and Order in it, have changed the circumstances under which Faith and Order works, but have not changed its purpose. We have become convinced that the time has come for a fuller statement of this purpose, and for a re-examination of the means by which Faith and Order should, within the World Council of Churches, seek its realization.

The Commission on Faith and Order understands that the unity which is both God's will and His gift to His Church is one which brings all in each place[4] who confess Christ Jesus as Lord into a fully committed fellowship with one another through one baptism into Him, holding the one apostolic faith, preaching the one Gospel and breaking the one bread, and having a corporate life reaching out in witness and service to all; and which at the same time unites them with the whole Christian fellowship in all places and all ages in such wise that

[3]As accepted by the Commission on Faith and Order and the Central Committee at St. Andrews 1960 and sent to the member churches for consideration and comment.

[4]The word "place" here is used both in its primary sense of local neighborhood and also under more modern conditions, of other areas in which Christians need to express unity in Christ, e.g. all those engaged in a local industry.

ministry and members are acknowledged by all, and that all can act and speak together as occasion requires for the tasks to which God calls the Church.

It is for such unity that we believe we must pray and work. Such a vision has indeed been the inspiration of the Faith and Order movement in the past, and we re-affirm that this is still our goal. We recognize that the brief definition of our objective which we have given above leaves many questions unanswered. In particular we would state emphatically that the unity we seek is not one of uniformity, nor a monolithic power structure, and that on the interpretation and the means of achieving certain of the matters specified in the preceding paragraph we are not yet of a common mind. The achievement of unity will involve nothing less than a death and rebirth for many forms of church life as we have known them. We believe that nothing less costly can finally suffice.

Having re-examined the tasks assigned to us in our Constitution, our place in the World Council and our ways of working, we now submit the following considerations and recommendations whereby we believe that we can best fulfil our responsibilities at this point in our history.

A. Scrutiny and re-assessment of our "functions" as set out in the Constitution of Faith and Order

(i) "To proclaim the essential oneness of the Church of Christ and to keep prominently before the World Council and the Churches the obligation to manifest that unity and its urgency for the work of evangelism"

It is our strong conviction that to proclaim the essential oneness of the Church of Christ involves facing the question "What kind of unity does God demand of His Church?" We agree that no one definition of the nature of unity can be a condition of membership in the WCC, but Faith and Order exists in order to stand for the unity of the Church as the will of God and for a ceaseless effort to know what obedience to that will means concretely. Only so can it be "manifest." The WCC can have no "neutrality" on whether that question is answered or not. Clearly the World Council is not in a position to say what the answer is in all its fulness; if it were, our quest for the "manifest unity" would already be at an end. As the Toronto Statement of 1950 put it: "As the conversation between the Churches develops, and as the Churches enter into closer contact with each other, they will no doubt have to face new decisions and problems. For the Council exists to break the deadlock between the Churches." (*ibid.* V. 2.) *All* the churches in the Council confront each other under the demand of God Himself that they should learn from Him the nature of the unity which we seek. It has been characteristic of Faith and Order to recognize that patience and thoroughness are needed for this task. But it is also necessary to recognize that in such matters we are not entirely free to proceed at our own pace, that events are forcing upon us various kinds of Christian co-operation, and that if we do not find true unity, we shall find ourselves remaining content with a form of organizational unity which leaves unfulfilled many of the central requirements of the Church's life. There is therefore need for a proper sense of urgency lest we lose the time that God gives us. Faith and Order must constantly press upon the Council and the churches the fact that the question of unity is one upon which an answer has to be given, and that to give no answer means to be shut up to the wrong answer. Specifically, Faith and Order must raise this question

(a) in Assemblies so far as its programme for the whole WCC allows;

(b) in Central Committee from time to time as best serves, as well as in the Theological Commissions which all at least bear upon the answer.

All these ways in which Faith and Order makes its witness within the WCC, but in order ultimately to reach the churches themselves, for whose sake all this activity is organized.

But within the Council, bearing in mind the WCC Constitution, it is also important that every department should be concerned that unity is borne in mind as it does its work, and we would hope that the WCC secretariat would, from time to time, ask how far their respective departments are contributing to the fullness of unity.

As plans for the integration with the International Missionary Council proceed, the relation of mission and unity should be more clearly seen. We would ask that national Christian councils and councils of churches should be asked whether their work also makes provision for Faith and Order, so that this connection may be brought home in every region.

As our Churches seek to obey God in the renewal of their confessional and liturgical life, and in promoting its mission, they will be deaf to what God is saying to them in our day if they do not, constantly and specifically, seek His guidance in how to translate all aspects of renewal and mission into manifestation of greater and growing unity.

Finally, in all this we must bring home the truth that our present differences and divisions hinder the mission and renewal of the Church and may obscure, even if they do not actually contradict, the Gospel of reconciliation.

(ii) "To study questions of faith, order, and worship with the relevant social, cultural, political, racial, and other factors in their bearing on the unity of the Church."

The content of our studies is of fundamental importance, and our first concern must be to ensure that Faith and Order is fully sensitive to the real questions which the Churches are asking, and to the questions which are yet scarcely articulate, so that its study is vitally related to their real needs. Study can be carried out in a great variety of ways. The traditional Faith and Order Theological Commission has a definite role where long-term co-operative study is needed. A serious question arises about the destination of such studies. We would distinguish today between:

(a) WCC Assemblies for

(i) Faith and Order witness at the heart of the WCC;

(ii) Communicating certain fruits of study.

Certain aspects of Theological Commissions' responsibilities can be discharged thus.

(b) *Special* Faith and Order Conferences (including world conferences) will also certainly be needed, because only in gatherings primarily concerned with Faith and Order issues is it possible for the fruits of preceding research to be fully shared, for there to be specific debate on the questions studied in the smaller groups of the Theological Commissions and for the themes for future study to emerge from the give-and-take of representative yet concentrated conference.

(c) Direct contact with the churches by the influence of delegates, staff visitation and correspondence, and by a careful programme for the dissemination of published material, both direct and through the churches and national councils.

But the Theological Commissions are by no means the only *method* of study nor existing themes its only *content*. Different *methods* suit different contents—e.g. field research, the short series of *ad hoc* conferences, regional enquiry on specific issues, fostering pilot-experiments in local groups, provision for theological faculties and other such special agencies to pay attention, as part of their own responsibilities, to Faith and Order issues.

Content is often also suggested by other Departments of the WCC. Faith and Order must be flexible to respond to such calls, e.g. the relation to unity of current discussions in other Departments, on the role of the laity and the ordination of women.

The ability to respond quickly to co-operation with other aspects of the WCC is indispensable if Faith and Order is to be, and to be felt to be, the organ of the WCC through which problems bearing upon the unity of the Church can be effectively dealt with when they reach the WCC from its member churches from any quarter whatsoever. It is clear that Faith and Order is not an oracle to *answer* all sorts of such questions, but it is the forum in which they can receive prompt and well-qualified consideration in a full ecumenical setting and in which the accumulation of experience of ecumenical work can be brought to bear upon them.

(iii) "To study the theological implications of the existence of the ecumenical movement."

The ecumenical movement in so far as it can rightly be called "the great new fact of our era" presents us with a work of God through His Spirit which we must seek to understand and interpret in our own generation. This is an aspect of the total "Mystery of the Church," but it contains specific issues sufficient to make it a distinguishable activity from (i) above, especially in the theological interpretation of such a fact as the WCC itself which, though it is not the Church, is certainly not unrelated to the Church and contains its own significance as a form of Christian unity which needs to be kept under theological scrutiny. The work begun by the Central Committee at Toronto in 1950 initiated a process which Faith and Order should feel a special responsibility to continue and to extend, for the sake both of those within the WCC and those beyond its membership.

(iv) "To study matters in the present relationships of the Churches to one another which cause difficulties and need theological clarification."

This function is not easily defined. One of its original consequences was a study of proselytism (later taken over by the Central Committee). But we believe that it marks out a territory of concrete and specific enquiries for which Faith and Order shall continue to be responsible.

(v) "To provide information concerning actual steps taken by the Churches towards reunion."

The furnishing of the churches with an accurate and up-to-date information service on reunion negotiations, and the research implied in collecting it, is a service in the direct line of Faith and Order interests which ought certainly to be fulfilled. Although we appreciate the extent to which the secretariat has been able to carry this out in recent years, we are convinced that it could only be done effectively if greater resources of staff were available.

As we have scrutinized these functions as defined in our present constitution, we wish to re-affirm our adherence to them, and to see them carried out with vigour. But we feel that the experience of the years since the Constitution was drafted would make us want to restate them for the future with some change of emphasis, expression and arrangement. Pending an appropriate moment for the revision of our Constitution, we content ourselves with this commentary upon their meaning.

B. SOME FURTHER IMPLICATIONS IN OUR WORK

We would go on to urge certain other concerns which we believe we are called by God to undertake, which, although not specifically indicated in our present terms of reference, are in keeping with the spirit and tradition of the Faith and Order movement.

(1) *Unity negotiations*

One of the striking consequences of nearly fifty years of Faith and Order work has been the creation of an atmosphere in which churches have been able to pass on from the discussion of unity in principle to negotiate concrete local unions. Nothing should impair the freedom of the churches themselves in this matter. But we would re-emphasize Constitution 4 (iv)[5] as meaning in

[5]"(iv) Only churches themselves are competent to take actual steps towards reunion by entering into negotiations with one another. The work of the movement is not to formulate schemes and tell the churches what they ought to do, but to act as the handmaid of the churches in the preparatory work of clearing away misunderstandings, discussing obstacles to reunion, and issuing reports which are submitted to the churches for their consideration."

our day that part of the "service" of Faith and Order must be to take a far more active attitude towards the various plans for unity without itself, of course, ever being the sponsor of any specific plan. But we believe we could and should serve the churches in the following ways:

(a) By providing for "consultations" as part of our own programme in which representatives of churches engaged in union negotiations could meet with each other and with a wide circle of those interested, to learn from each other and to see their own negotiations in a wider context. The gratitude expressed for the "unofficial consultations" already held encourages us to make them in future a more direct responsibility of Faith and Order whenever its own meetings draw together a widely representative gathering which includes such interests.

(b) By analyzing the various schemes in current discussion, with a view to discovering the bearing which each may have on other negotiations and the solutions of difficulties found in them which may be useful to other churches discussing union.

(c) If inter-church consultations of the kind contemplated in paragraph (a) above should lead to invitations to the Faith and Order Commission to assist at any point in unity negotiations, the officers of the Commission should regard themselves as empowered to designate competent persons to serve as consultants, with the understanding that these consultants do not speak in the name of the Commission as a whole. The officers should also be ready to provide relevant material from the experience of the Commission. It is hoped that this readiness to render any assistance called for will become known to the churches.

(2) *Regional work and other meetings* which are less than fully comprehensive Faith and Order Conferences. By an action of the Faith and Order Working Committee at Davos in 1955, endorsed by the Central Committee in the same year, the Faith and Order Commission interprets para. 4 of its Constitution as allowing meetings which are not based on invitations "addressed to Christian Churches throughout the world."

The success of the New Zealand and Oberlin Conferences, of the Lutheran-Reformed meetings in Europe, and the Indian regional conference, leads us to mention here gatherings of this kind as being in future part of our regular concern. In particular we would hope that many groups who find themselves in a small minority at our normal conferences could sometimes be afforded opportunities to meet in a setting in which they would be relieved of some of the disadvantages and inhibitions of appearing always as a minority.

We would also consider whether other groups than churches actually negotiating should be drawn into contact with each other—e.g., churches resulting from union negotiations to meet with representatives from some of the world confessional organizations with which their component churches are related; or, certain churches in a particular area be invited to enter into conversation on Faith and Order themes.

In this context, we would like to stress the value of active Faith and Order departments in national Christian councils and councils of churches, with which the Faith and Order secretariat is glad to co-operate. Local pilot schemes of study, under Faith and Order auspices, could occasionally be arranged in consultation with the national council concerned.

(3) *Relations with Christians outside the WCC membership*

One of our basic principles is to draw churches out of isolation into conference. In this connection, we believe that we have a responsibility, in this time in which our member churches have been able to overcome that isolation by meeting in the WCC, especially towards those churches which have chosen not to avail themselves of that particular opportunity. We also note that we are empowered to invite representatives of such churches to serve in our Commission (v. Constitution, para. 5 (ii)b), and so, by implication, on our Theological Commissions.

We have especially in mind two groups among those who "accept Our Lord Jesus Christ as God and Saviour."

(a) *The Roman Catholic Church* constitutes so large a part of Christendom that we are bound to take it into consideration in our work for Christian unity. But we realize the very serious difficulties which arise, both from their side and from ours, to hinder any official or clearly defined relationship. Yet Faith and Order is an aspect of the WCC in which the Roman Catholic Church has shown an interest. Roman Catholic theologians have made important contributions by their writings to the discussion of Faith and Order issues. We believe that this theological discussion should be pursued in whatever ways may be mutually acceptable.

(b) *Protestant Churches* outside the WCC need another form of approach, for as compared with the unity (though complex) of the Roman Catholic Church, we are here dealing with very diverse entities. But we believe that many are ready to enter into common study with the WCC and to meet in personal contact in various countries and regions. They comprise another group of fellow Christians with whom Faith and Order should enter into fellowship on the ground of common concern for Christian mission and unity.

With regard to them both, we would urge that Faith and Order should:

(i) aim at a situation in the WCC staff which ensured that there should always be people sufficiently free from other commitments to make it a first charge on their time to be in continuous, personal, and well-informed contact with the whole complexity of both these groups;

(ii) on the basis of such contact, the Faith and Order Secretariat, Working Committee and other groups in Faith and Order would be in a position to be kept informed of developments and openings, and so able to seek their participation in our theological work where it was then deemed possible and advisable.

C. Consequences for Organization

Our deepest concern is that the World Council as a whole should always serve that unity into which God calls His People to be reconciled through His Son. As partial consequences of responding to that call, our separated churches have found in the WCC an organ through which to do many things together, and for all of this we give thanks to God. We believe that all the tasks we have outlined, and others which we trust that He will show us, together constitute a central part of the Council's work, and an ingredient in the whole which keeps all our churches aware of the full unity of Word and Sacrament, Ministry and Mission, in universal and local fellowship.

We believe that in order for the World Council as a whole to be this effective organ in the cause of unity, Faith and Order should be at the centre of its life and a major element in its organizational structure. We fully recognize that the WCC is a complex organism which has total problems of finance and structural development and has many concerns to reckon with. The Constitution of the World Council itself, however, makes it clear that Faith and Order is to have a peculiarly central position in its life: "The functions of the World Council shall be: (i) to carry on the work of the world movements for Faith and

Order and for Life and Work . . . The World Council shall discharge part of its functions by the appointment of Commissions. . . . There shall be a Faith and Order Commission. . . ." It is our conviction that not only to enable Faith and Order to accomplish its specific tasks within the total work of the WCC, and more particularly, to promote the original intention of the founding of the WCC that the concern for unity should be at the very heart of its life and penetrate all of its activities, the structural position of Faith and Order in the organization of the WCC needs to be reinforced as well as its staff and financial resources strengthened.

Considering the original purposes of the WCC as outlined in the Constitution, the following proposals are considered by this Commission not to involve any radical change in the relation of Faith and Order to the WCC but simply a logical development of a pattern which is already provided for in the Constitution and a natural strengthening of Faith and Order within the WCC commensurate with the growth and development of the World Council itself in recent years.

The Commission on Faith and Order has examined not only its own role within the WCC but also the internal organization of the Commission itself. In this connection we believe it to be necessary to clarify the meaning and implications of membership in the Faith and Order Commission. Each member should be given a clear understanding of his responsibilities towards the Faith and Order Commission and towards his own Church; and leaders of churches should be fully cognizant of the fact they are represented in the Faith and Order Commission so that they may be disposed to appropriate the experience of such members and give them due support. Moreover it may prove necessary to re-examine the manner in which such members are added to the Faith and Order Commission in the light of requirements imposed by its future tasks.

Our discussion on the future of Faith and Order carried on now for four years and comments received on our Interim Report have made it clear that the following provisions should be made:

(1) The place of Faith and Order as a constituent Commission of the WCC, as provided for in the WCC Constitution, should be clarified so that it has a place and role appropriate to the central importance of the concern for church unity in the life of the WCC. The Commission has given earnest consideration as to how this may be achieved, including the specific sug-

gestion that Faith and Order take the form of a Division after the next Assembly. Aware of certain serious difficulties which this would raise, and recognizing that the Central Committee must weigh this problem in the light of the overall situation and decide what may be recommended to the Faith and Order Commission and submitted to the Assembly, we have requested the Committee to consider this suggestion or others which might occur to the Committee, and to respond with its advice as to the ways and means by which the concerns of Faith and Order may best be realized. Though the Central Committee itself has not yet been in a position to respond to our request, its Programme and Finance Committee in its Final Report has done so in the following words:

> At the present stage the Committee considers that in the light of the total situation in the WCC and in view of the importance of study in the programme of Faith and Order, the Commission or its Working Committee should continue to be represented on the Committee of the Division of Studies and the Secretariat should continue to work, as at present, under the authority of the Constitution of Faith and Order and within the Division of Studies.

With this suggestion we concur at this time, though we believe that the location of Faith and Order within the Study Division is not the best final solution to our problem. Whatever decisions are taken by the Central Committee, now or eventually, we believe that close liaison should be maintained in the realm of study with other departments through the proposed Staff Coordinating Committee on Study in which all WCC departments are represented.

(2) There should be a report to the Central Committee every year, prepared by the Faith and Order Working Committee, on current issues and developments in the field of Christian unity. This is supported by the Final Report of the Programme and Finance Committee:

The Committee recommends that time be afforded by the Central Committee for a report each year by Faith and Order on general developments or specific issues in the realm of unity.

(3) There continue to be made in every WCC Assembly the same generous provision as has been allowed hitherto for discussion upon issues of unity.

(4) World Conferences specifically on Faith and Order have

an irreplaceable role and provision needs to be made for them from time to time.

(5) The programme we have outlined above also clearly implies a larger staff than is at present available. The distribution and character of the work to be done depends upon the qualities of the persons involved. The Faith and Order staff should always represent in themselves as wide a range as possible of confessional and national traditions. The programme outlined in the earlier part of this report would fully occupy a staff whose duties could be illustrated in such a picture as this:

(a) *Director of the Commission on Faith and Order,* who would be responsible for carrying out general strategy of Faith and Order work as well as being intimately involved in the working out of general WCC policy at the highest level. He would be responsible for the general co-ordination of the Faith and Order programme. He would also be particularly concerned with the extension of Faith and Order activities in new areas as well as having general oversight over the consultative service for church union negotiations. He would also have special responsibility for these suggested contacts with non-member churches.

(b) *Executive Secretary,* who would be responsible for the continuing programme of Faith and Order as carried on through the Faith and Order Commission, the long-term Theological Commissions, and for the general administration involved in these as well as for Conferences and Consultations, and for the promotion of Faith and Order studies among the member churches.

(c) *Research Secretary,* who would carry on special research and survey projects, and in particular would be responsible for surveys, both factual and analytical, of church union schemes.

(6) The Director of Faith and Order needs to have the closest relationship with the WCC General Secretariat and, to be fully involved in the total work of the WCC, should be a member of the Staff Executive Group[6] as the Final Report of the Programme and Finance Committee recommends. We also recommend that

[6]The Staff Executive Group consists of the General Secretary, the four Associate General Secretaries, the Director of Finance, and the Director of Information.

he be given the title: Theological Secretary of the World Council of Churches. This title is reminiscent of former Faith and Order usage. It does not imply that other World Council Secretaries have not been and are not to be chosen for their theological competence, but recognizes the unique responsibilities attaching to this post.

We believe that in these ways Faith and Order would be more clearly seen to occupy a place in the structure of the WCC which properly reflects its central and fundamental role in the whole ecumenical movement.

For the proposed generous increase in the budget of Faith and Order recommended by the Programme and Finance Committee we are most grateful, and believe that this will go far to make possible another recommendation of that Committee:

That other arrangements to strengthen the regular operation of the Commission be developed.

To this task we propose to set ourselves.

IV.

Faith and Order
Publications

1.

THE GREAT CONFERENCES

Preparatory Material,

Reports, Comments, etc.

The list of the numbered Faith and Order papers is to be consulted also.

Lausanne:

Faith and Order, Proceedings of the World Conference, Lausanne, August 3-21, 1927, ed. H. N. Bate, New York, 1928.

Can the churches unite? Issued under the auspices of the World Conference on Faith and Order, New York, 1927.

Convictions, A Selection from the Responses of the Churches to . . . Lausanne, 1927; ed. Leonard Hodgson, London, 1934.

Lang, August: Die Weltkirchenkonferenz in Lausanne. Drei Vorträge, Halle, 1927.

Laun, Justus Ferdinand: Die Konferenz von Lausanne. Berichte, Ergebnisse, Aufgaben, Gotha, 1928.

Martin, Alfred von: Die Welkirchenkonferenz von Lausanne, Stuttgart, 1928.

Pribilla, Max: Um kirchliche Einheit. Stockholm—Lausanne—Rom, Freiburg, 1929.

Report of the Committee appointed by the Archbishops of Canterbury and York to consider the findings of the Lausanne Conference on Faith and Order, London, 1930.

Söderblom, Nathan: Randbemerkungen zu Lausanne, Gütersloh, 1928.
Soper, Edmund Davison: Lausanne: the will to understand, New York, 1928.
Woods, E. S.: Lausanne 1927, An Interpretation of the World Conference on Faith and Order, London, 1927.

Edinburgh:

The Doctrine of Grace, ed. W. T. Whitley, with an introduction by the Archbishop of York, London, 1932.
Die Kirche Jesu Christi und das Wort Gottes. Ein Studienbuch über das Wort Gottes als Lebensgrund und Lebensform der Kirche; ed. W. Zoellner and W. Stählin, Berlin, 1937.
Stählin, Wilhelm, Von göttlichen Geheimnis, Kassel, 1936. The Mystery of God. Transl. by R. Birch Hoyle. Prefaces by A. E. Garvie and W. Zoellner. Publ. for the World Conference on Faith and Order, London, 1937.
The Ministry and the Sacraments. Report of the Theological Commission appointed by the Continuation Committee of the Faith and Order Movement under the Chairmanship of the Rt. Rev. A. C. Headlam; ed. R. Dunkerley, London, 1937.
Douglass, H. Paul: A decade of objective progress in church unity 1927-37. Report No. 4; prepared by the Commission on the Church's unity in Life and Worship (Comm. IV) for the World Conference on Faith and Order, Edinburgh, 1937. New York and London, 1937.
The Second World Conference on Faith and Order held at Edinburgh, August 3-18, 1937; ed. Leonard Hodgson, London, 1938.
Dun, Angus: Studies on Church Unity, with primary reference to the Report of the Second World Conference on Faith and Order, Edinburgh, 1937. New York, 1938.
Martin, Hugh: Edinburgh 1937. The Story of the Second World Conference on Faith and Order, London, 1937.
Nikolaos, Metropolit Axomes: Diaskepsis Edimburgu (Greek) Kairo, 1938.
Palmer, Edwin James: The Cost of Reunion. A Speech made at the Edinburgh Conference on Faith and Order 1937 and an Epilogue to that Conference, London, 1937.
Wissing, J. C.: De Kerk aan het Werk in Oxford en Edinburg., 's Gravenhage, 1939.

Amsterdam:

Man's Disorder and God's Design. The Amsterdam Assembly Series, Vol. 1: The Universal Church in God's Design, Vol. 5: The First Assembly of the World Council of Churches held at Amsterdam, August 22—September 4, 1948; ed. W. A. Visser 't Hooft, London, 1949.

Lund:

The Nature of the Church. Papers presented to the Theological Commission appointed by the Continuation Committee of the World Conference on Faith and Order; ed. R. Newton Flew, London, 1952.

Ways of Worship. The Report of a Theological Commission of Faith and Order; ed. Pehr Edwall, Eric Hayman, William D. Maxwell, London, 1951.

Intercommunion. The Report of the Theological Commission appointed by the Continuation Committee of the World Conference on Faith and Order together with a Selection from the Material presented to the Commission; ed. by Donald Baillie and John Marsh, London, 1952.

Dodd, C. H.; Cragg, G. R.; Ellul, Jacques: Social and Cultural Factors in Church Divisions. With . . . report of a Conference held at the Ecumenical Institute at Bossey, 1951, London/New York, 1952.

The Third World Conference on Faith and Order held at Lund, August 15-28, 1952; ed. Oliver S. Tomkins, London, 1953.

Ecumenical Review, V, 1 (Oct., 1952) and 2 (Jan., 1953). Robertson, E. H.: *Lund, 1952.* London, 1962.

Evanston:

The Christian Hope and the Task of the Church. Six ecumenical Surveys and The Report to the Assembly prepared by the Advisory Commission on the Main Theme, 1954. New York, 1954.

The Evanston Report. The Second Assembly of the World Council of Churches 1954; ed. W. A. Visser 't Hooft, New York, 1955.

New Delhi:

"Die Einheit, die wir suchen" (W. Joest, W. Kreck, W. Küppers), Oekumenische Rundschau, X, 3, 1961.

Consultation on Services of Holy Communion at Ecumenical Gatherings held at Bossey, 1961; Ecumenical Review XIII, 3 April, 1961.

Evanston to New Delhi. Report of the Central Committee to the Third Assembly, Geneva, 1961.

Work Book for the Assembly Committees prepared for the Third Assembly of the World Council of Churches, Geneva, 1961.

New Delhi Speaks, London and New York, 1962.

2.

OFFICIAL NUMBERED PUBLICATIONS, SERIES 1, 1910-1948

1. 1910 Joint Commission Appointed to Arrange for a World Conference on Faith and Order. (Report and Resolution of the Protestant Episcopal Church suggesting the Conference and Report and Resolutions of National Council of the Congregational Churches.) 8 p.

2. 1910 Joint Commission Appointed to Arrange for a World Conference on Faith and Order. (Report and Resolution of the Protestant Episcopal Church suggesting the Conference.) 8 p.

3. 1911 Report of the Committee on Plan and Scope. 20 p.

12. The World Conference and the Problem of Unity, by the Rev. Francis J. Hall, D.D. 30 p.

13. Virorum Congressui Omnium Gentium de Fide et Ordine Instituendo Communiter Delectorum Ad Concilium Episcopale Ecclesiarum Catholicarum Veterum Europaearum Epistola. (Letter to the Council of the Old Catholic Churches in Europe. In Latin, with English translation.) 16 p.

14. 1912 An official statement by the Joint Commission of the Protestant Episcopal Church in the United States of America. 18 p.

15. 1913 Prayer and Unity. By a Layman. 32 p.
16. Questions of Faith and Order for Consideration by the Proposed Conference, by the Rt. Rev. A. C. A. Hall, D.D. 14 p.
17. Bibliography of Topics Related to Church Unity, compiled by Rev. Francis J. Hall, D.D. 24 p.
18. 1913 Unity or Union: Which? by the Rt. Rev. P. M. Rhinelander, D.D. 24 p.
19. 1913 The Conference Spirit. By a Layman. 32 p.
20. 1913 The Manifestation of Unity, by the Rt. Rev. C. P. Anderson, D.D. 48 p.
21. 1913 List of commissions Already Appointed. 22 p.
    1914 Revised with additional appointments, in successive editions.
    1915, 1917, 1919, 1920, 1920, 1920, 1922, 1923, 1924, 1925, 1925, 1926
23. 1913 Report of the Joint Commission to the General Convention of the Protestant Episcopal Church, 1913.
    36 p.
24. 1913 A First Preliminary Conference. 54 p.
25. 1913 Report of the Committee on Church Unity of the National Council of Congregational Churches, 1913.
    16 p.
26. 1914 A World Movement for Christian Unity. By the Rev. Lefferd M. A. Haughwout. 22 p.
27. 1914 Second Meeting of the Advisory Committee. Report of the Second Deputation to Great Britain. The Call for a Truce of God. 46 p.
28. 1915 The Object and Method of Conference. 36 p.
29. 1915 A Manual of Prayer for Unity. 40 p.
30. 1916 North American Preparatory Conference, Garden City, Long Island, New York, U.S.A., January 4-6, 1916. Report of Progress by the Secretary. Opening Address by the Rt. Rev. C. P. Anderson, D.D. 30 p.
31. 1916 Report of the Joint Commission to the General Convention of the Protestant Episcopal Church. 36 p.
32. 1919 Report of the Deputation to Europe and the East.
    38 p.
33. 1920 Report of the Preliminary Meeting at Geneva, Switzerland, August 12-20, 1920. A Pilgrimage Toward Unity.
    96 p.
34. 1921 A Compilation of Proposals for Christian Unity. 80 p.

Committee, Committee of reference, Committee of Theologians, and Business Committee. 32 p.

64. Continuation Committee of the World Conference on Faith and Order. Report on the Responses from the Churches to the Lausanne Reports, Presented to the Committee at Mürren, August, 1930. 20 p.

65. Records of the Continuation Committee of the World Conference on Faith and Order, High Leigh, Hoddesdon, England, August 18-21, 1931. 28 p.

66. 1931 Report of the Theological Committee, 19th August 1931, The Theology of Grace. 32 p.

67. 1931 The Lausanne Movement. 12 p.

68. 1932 Outline Minutes of the Executive Committee, High Leigh, August 31-September 1, 1932. 8 p.

69. 1933 Membership Lists. 36 p.

70. 1933 The Lausanne Movement: Its Past, Present and Future. 16 p.

71. The 1934 Meeting of the Continuation Committee Held at Hertenstein, Switzerland, September 3-6. 44 p.

72. 1935 Reports of Local Discussion Groups, 1933-1934. 42 p.

73. The 1935 Meeting of the Continuation Committee Held at Hindsgaul, Middlefart, Denmark, August 4-7. 28 p.

74. 1935 Programme for the Second World Conference on Faith and Order to be Held at Edinburgh, Scotland, August 3-18, 1937. 16 p.

75. 1935 Delegates Appointed to Represent their Churches at the Second World Conference to be Held at Edinburgh, August 3-18, 1937. 18 p.
Revised editions in 1936 and 1937.

76. 1936 Some Prolegomena to the 1937 World Conference. 46 p.

77. 1936 From Lausanne to Edinburgh, A Syllabus for Study-Groups. 20 p.

78. 1936 A List of Recommended Books. 12 p.

79. 1936 The 1936 Meeting of the Continuation Committee held at St. George's School, Clarens, Switzerland, August 31-September 3, 1936. 40 p.

80. Constitution of the Second World Conference to be held at Edinburgh, August 3-18, 1937. 4 p.

81. 1937 Report of Commission III appointed by the 1927 Continuation Committee in preparation for the Second

World Conference to be held at Edinburgh in 1937. The Ministry and Sacraments. 46 p.

3.

NUMBERED PUBLICATIONS, SERIES 2, BEGINNING 1948

1. Continuation Committee—World Council of Churches' Commission on Faith and Order: Meetings at Amsterdam and Baarn, Holland, August-September 1948.

   This pamphlet is No. 103 of the First Series, as containing the record of the final meeting of the Edinburgh Continuation Committee, at Amsterdam, August 21, 1948. It is also No. 1 of the Second Series, as including the record of the first meeting, at Baarn, September 7-8, 1948, of the same body in its new capacity as the Commission on Faith and Order of the World Council.

2. Meeting at Chichester, England, July 16th to 20th 1949. Minutes of the Commission meeting.

3. *The Church in the Purpose of God by Oliver S. Tomkins. An introduction to the work of the Commission in preparation for the Third World Conference on Faith and Order to be held at Lund, Sweden, in 1952.* 1950

4. Executive Committee. Minutes of meeting held at Bièvres, France, September 9th-11th, 1950.

5. *Intercommunion. A Report of a Theological Commission in preparation for Lund.* May 1951

6. *Ways of Worship. A Report of a Theological Commission in preparation for Lund.* 1951

234

7. *The Church. A Report of a Theological Commission in preparation for Lund.* 1951

8. Meetings of the Commission and of the Executive Committee at Clarens, Switzerland, August 13-17, 1951.

9. Minutes of meeting held at Lambeth Palace, London, from January 30th to February 1st, 1952 (Meeting of Executive Committee).

10. *Social and Cultural Factors in Church Divisions by C. H. Dodd, G. R. Cragg, Jacques Ellul.* With a Preface by Oliver Tomkins and the Report of a Conference held at the Ecumenical Institute at Bossey in November 1951. 1952 American Edition: *More Than Doctrine Divides the Churches.* A study of the nontheological (social and cultural) factors in church divisions.

11. *Towards Church Union 1937-1952* by Stephen C. Neill. A survey of Approaches to closer Union among the Churches. 1952

11a *Survey of Church Union Negotiations* by J. Robert Nelson. Article reprinted from *The Ecumenical Review* for April 1954, as a supplement to Bishop Neill's survey.

11b *Survey of Church Union Negotiations.* Reprinted from *The Ecumenical Review*, Vol. VIII No. 1, October 1955.

11c *Survey of Church Union Negotiations.* Reprinted from *The Ecumenical Review*, Vol. IX, No. 3, April 1957.

12. Third World Conference on Faith and Order, Lund, August 15-29, 1952. *Official Handbook.*

13. The Third World Conference on Faith and Order, Lund 1952. *Who's Who. Wer Ist's? Qui êtes-vous?*, Revised edition; and *List of Delegates* appointed by their churches together with others attending the Conference. 1952.

14. Minutes of the Meeting of the Commission on Faith and Order, together with the Minutes of the first meeting of the Working Committee on August 28th, 1952, at Lund, Sweden.

15. *Report of the Third World Conference on Faith and Order, Lund, Sweden; August 15-28, 1952.*

16. Members of the Faith and Order Commission elected at the Lund Conference 1952, and the Secretariat of the Commission. May, 1953.

17. Working Committee. Minutes of meeting held at the Château de Bossey, near Geneva, 11th to 19th August, 1953.

18. *Faith and Order—Our Oneness in Christ and our Disunity as Churches. An Ecumenical Survey prepared under the auspices of the World Council of Churches.*

19. *Faith and Order; Finding our Oneness*
    One of a series of popular pamphlets on the various Departments of the World Council of Churches.

20. *Faith and Order—Our Oneness in Christ and our Disunity as Churches. A Report from the Second Assembly of the World Council of Churches; Evanston, Ill., U.S.A., August 15-31, 1954.*

21. Minutes, Commission and Working Committee, Evanston and Chicago, 1954.

22. Minutes, Working Committee, Davos, 25-30 July, 1955.

23. Minutes, Working Committee, Herrenalb, 17-20 July, 1956.

24. *Responses of the Churches to the Report of the Lund Conference. 1957.*

25. Minutes, Commission and Working Committee, New Haven, Conn., U.S.A., 20-25 July, 1957.

26. Minutes, Working Committee, Geneva, 15-20 July, 1958.

27. Minutes, Working Committee, Spittal, Austria, August 1959.

28. Survey of Church Union Negotiations 1957-1959. (Offprint from *The Ecumenical Review*, Vol. XII No. 2, January 1960.) (Continuation from No. 11c.)

29. *One Lord, One Baptism. Report on the Divine Trinity and the Unity of the Church and Report on the Meaning of Baptism, by the Theological Commission on Christ and the Church.* SCM Press, Ltd., London, 1960. American edition: Augsburg Publishing House, Minneapolis.

30. *Orthodoxy—a Faith and Order Dialogue.* (Offprint from *The Ecumenical Review.* Vol. XII, No. 2, January 1960.)

31. Minutes, Faith & Order Commission, St. Andrews, Scotland, 3-8 August, 1960.

32. Law, Polity and the Reunion of the Church, by William Stringfellow (reprinted from *The Ecumenical Review* Vol. XIII, No. 3, April, 1961)

33. Minutes of the Working Committee meeting, Geneva, 16-19 June, 1961.

34. *The Old and the New in the Church. Report on Tradition and Traditions: Report on Institutionalism and Unity.* SCM Press: (Studies in Ministry and Worship, 18), London, 1961. American edition: Published by Augsburg Publishing House, Minneapolis, U.S.A.
35. Survey of Church Union Negotiations 1959-1961. (Offprint from *The Ecumenical Review*, Vol. XIV, No. 3, April 1962.) (Continuation from No. 28.)

INDEX

239

241

242

244

245